Pr

TWO-TIME WINNER OF THE GILLER PRIZE
WINNER OF THE GOVERNOR GENERAL'S LITERARY AWARD
WINNER OF THE COMMONWEALTH FIRST BOOK PRIZE
WINNER OF THE BRESSANI PRIZE

"M.G. Vassanji's style—diverse and playful—brings the reader along effortlessly, illuminating the ramshackle roots of self, family, and culture."
—Governor General's Literary Award Jury

"The seductive power of Vassanji's prose mesmerizes. . . . One of Canada's best novelists." —*Quill & Quire*

"[Vassanji's] material is so compelling that he needs little more than to adopt the role of a chronicler. . . . A humble village, in the imagination of this chronicler, becomes a vortex of varying belief systems and ways of life." —*National Post*

"One of the strengths of Vassanji's writing is how he demonstrates—not in a gratuitously cynical way but through insightful stories about specific individuals—that even sensitive, self-aware people can become trapped in a skein of historical wrongs. . . . Vassanji's body of work is a gentle reminder of the fluidity of history—and of the ability of an individual to belong to many places and be many things at the same time." —*The Hindu*

"To little intimacies as to larger histories, Vassanji is a discerning and sensitive guide." —*Winnipeg Free Press*

"Gorgeous and heart-rending. . . . Vassanji explores [love and loss] with all the tact of a true literary power." —*Chicago Tribune*

Also by the Author

FICTION

Everything There Is

What You Are

A Delhi Obsession

Nostalgia

The Magic of Saida

The Assassin's Song

When She Was Queen

The In-Between World of Vikram Lall

Amriika

The Book of Secrets

Uhuru Street

No New Land

The Gunny Sack

NON-FICTION

And Home Was Kariakoo

A Place Within: Rediscovering India

Mordecai Richler

Nowhere, Exactly

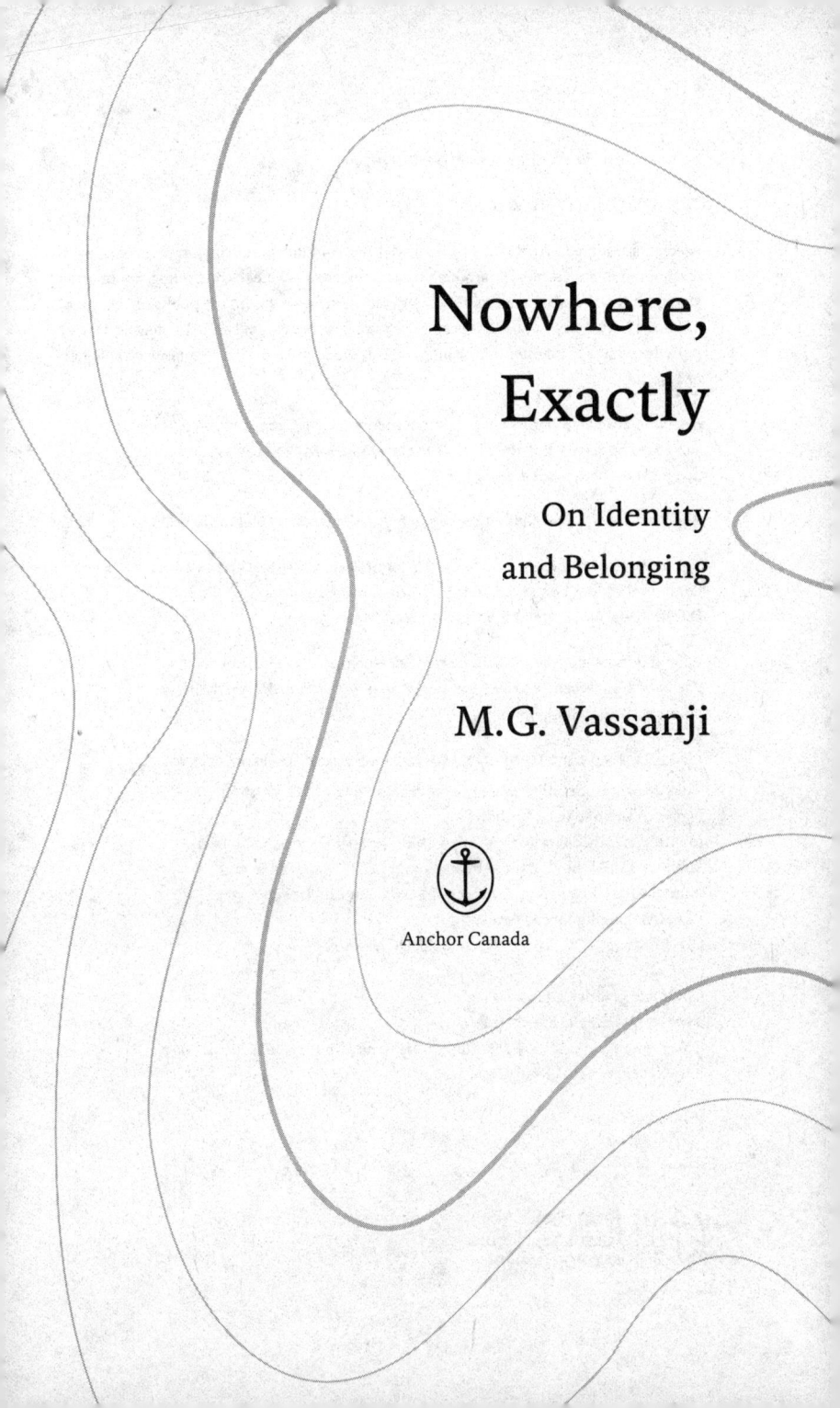

On Identity and Belonging

M.G. Vassanji

Anchor Canada

PUBLISHED IN 2025 BY ANCHOR CANADA

Copyright © 2024 M.G. Vassanji

All rights reserved. No part of this book may be reproduced, scanned, transmitted, or distributed in any form or by any electronic or mechanical means, including information storage and retrieval systems, without permission in writing from the publisher, except by a reviewer, who may quote brief passages in a review. No part of this book may be used or reproduced in any manner for the purpose of training artificial intelligence technologies or systems.

Anchor Canada, an imprint of Penguin Random House Canada Limited, 320 Front Street West, Suite 1400, Toronto, Ontario, M5V 3B6, Canada
penguinrandomhouse.ca

Anchor Canada and colophon are registered trademarks of Penguin Random House LLC.

The authorized representative in the EU for product safety and compliance is Penguin Random House Ireland, Morrison Chambers, 32 Nassau Street, Dublin, D02 YH68, Ireland, https://eu-contact.penguin.ie

Epigraph translation of the Brihadaranyaka Upanishad by Patrick Olivelle, *The Early Upanisads: Annotated text and translation* (Oxford University Press [South Asia research], 1998), 73.

LIBRARY AND ARCHIVES CANADA CATALOGUING IN PUBLICATION

Title: Nowhere, exactly : on identity and belonging / M.G. Vassanji.
Names: Vassanji, M. G., author.
Identifiers: Canadiana 20230524869 | ISBN 9780385697729 (softcover)
Subjects: LCSH: Immigrants—Psychology. | LCSH: Emigration and immigration—Psychological aspects. | LCSH: Identity (Psychology) | LCSH: Belonging (Social psychology)
Classification: LCC JV6013 .V37 2025 | DDC 304.801/9—dc23

Cover and text design by Lisa Jager
Typeset by Daniella Zanchetta
Cover images: (house) V. J. Matthew, (lines) Theus, both Adobe Stock Images; (city) IgorSPb/iStock/Getty Images

Printed in Canada

2 4 6 8 9 7 5 3 1

In Memoriam
Firoz Manji
Better late than never

About this self (atman), one can only say "not—, not—" (neti neti). He is ungraspable, for he cannot be grasped. He is undecaying, for he is not subject to decay. He has nothing sticking to him, for he does not stick to anything.

Brihadaranyaka Upanishad

    And I have known the eyes already, known them all—
The eyes that fix you in a formulated phrase,
And when I am formulated, sprawling on a pin,
When I am pinned and wriggling on the wall,
Then how should I begin
To spit out all the butt-ends of my days and ways?
    And how should I presume?

T.S. Eliot, "The Love Song of J. Alfred Prufrock"

Contents

Introduction 1

1. Nowhere Anywhere 7
2. Voices in the Wilderness: The Nowhere Artist 21
3. The Canadian Identity, or Lack Thereof 41
4. Patriotism and Loyalty 63
5. Writing to Somebody, Somewhere: The Telling Is Not Easy 78
6. Nowhere in Africa 87
7. Am I a Canadian Writer? 101
8. Nowhere with God: Uneasy Confessions of a Syncretist 115
9. Gandhi: Discovery and Reappraisal 141
10. The Urge to Get Away: Finding India 162
11. So As Not to Die: The Need to Remember 181
12. Lawrence Durrell and I: The View Across the Street 199
13. Whose War? A Blasphemous Suggestion 217
14. A New Dispensation? After George Floyd 223
15. Cinderella on the Outside 238

Endnotes 247
Acknowledgements 261

Introduction

Ever since, just out of my teens, I left my hometown Dar es Salaam, Tanzania to study abroad, I have carried within me a profound sense of loss and uncertainty regarding who I was, where I had come from, and what I had become. I recall telling myself, during my first weeks on this continent, Don't forget. As the months and years went by, I could not escape the feeling that I belonged[1] to more places than one, with the resultant uneasy sense of guilt and betrayal. Memory—personal and familial, historical and ancestral, of the old and the recent—was stretching me out across continents and cultures. In Toronto now I feel completely at home;[2] having paid my dues as a new arrival and an alien, I now know it with an intimacy and a possessiveness that any settled citizen would feel entitled to; it is the place where I am the most comfortable and feel the safest. It is where I return to, the house in North Toronto. I have crossed Canada coast to coast by road and rail, visited its cities many times over. The thoughts and arguments collected here testify to my belongingness. And yet whenever I set foot on the ground in Dar es Salaam, there's a spring in my step, a lift in my spirit; my language, my tone, my relationships with people are different; there is a sense of ease. And when I arrive in India—though I first went there only well into my maturity—a voice inside me says that this too is a homecoming—despite its current wave of religious nationalism that would possibly spurn my claim.

Am I disloyal to Canada? Have I been disloyal to Tanzania, choosing to stay away when I had left it with a vow to return and contribute to this developing nation that nurtured me? There was a time not long ago when the answers to both these questions would have been strongly in the affirmative. For long I was nagged by this doubt about my honesty—professing one thing, while harbouring qualifiers. But the passing decades have presented me with two ameliorative viewpoints, healing thoughts.

We live now in times of massive migrations, rapidly changing demographics, instant communication over distances that once seemed forbidding. (When I left home, a letter from there took two weeks to arrive.) Canada in particular does not demand amnesia. So I would like to think. Racially restricted once, it is now diverse and much more liberal than before. A large percentage of its people were born elsewhere or are descendants of such people. This new reality and the positive attitudes to it have become the defining strengths of this country. I have brought up a family here. At the same time, the part of the world I come from and which beckons me has also changed. A new generation has sprung up there, nurtured on social media, not quite as familiar with or sensitive to the concerns that preoccupied their elders so passionately in the newly independent country; it does not need me. The country may take some comfort in my loyalty and my representing it and defending it, in however limited a fashion, in the literary universe. If I could not teach or heal or build there, as I had hoped in my youth, I have made my modest contribution by writing about it and adding to its memories. And it remains indelibly a part of my identity.

Canada today is in many ways a far cry from the country I came to in 1980—mixed and democratically idealistic on the surface, segregated at its heart. It is now more and more recognized—by governments and citizens—that the different races and cultures that belong to it are all equally part of the national fabric; that some are not more privileged than others because of European ancestry or "founding" status—a concept whose perversity has become evident in recent times, as historical wrongs get increasingly acknowledged. These changes in attitude have been highlighted, perhaps accelerated by the dramatic discoveries of Indigenous Peoples' graves in Canada and the protests that resulted from a series of new police shootings of Black people in the United States. How deep these changes will go, erasing attitudes inherited from centuries of racism and imperial domination, remains to be seen.

When I think of art and culture, identity and belonging have presented an even deeper conundrum. A nation's culture has deep roots in the past—which is why nationalist demagogues everywhere take hold of historical symbols to make their exclusive stands. Western countries not only claim cultural roots in European antiquity but also possess a lateral continuity with each other across the Atlantic in shared experiences and memory. The white Canadian artist—someone of European descent—is conscious of this continuity, works within and adds to it. Canadian art has long sought endorsement and inspiration from Europe and America. How does a poet or novelist, a musician or painter arrived from another culture, fit into it? Am I a Canadian writer, or an African one, or an Indian one? I have been called all three, and have been denied as any of the three. I have also been faulted for not being a hundred percent one or another. Toronto bookstores don't seem to know where to place me. In a pure sense, in an artistic sense, it does not matter. Creative inspiration does not come waving a national flag. A writer writes, that's it. *Bas*, as we used to say. But that's simplistic. An artist cannot survive in isolation for long; like an unseen planet in an unknown galaxy he might as well not exist.

Assimilate! is a cry often heard. Few people understand what that entails. Assimilation is not a simple, one-way process, for I bring along cultures, histories, and experiences from elsewhere that do not have European roots. For every upheaval in Europe or America one can point to another in Asia or Africa; for every epic or legendary hero in the West there are numerous elsewhere. For Athens or Rome there are Damascus, Cairo, Beijing, Delhi, Timbuctoo, Zimbabwe, and more. For someone like me to find a place in that continuum of which Canada is a part, it has to make room for me; it has to adjust its position. Together we must evolve. My memories will fade and new ones form; they will evolve into new thoughts and structures. And this country will accommodate a bigger world, a bigger history. But will it?

INTRODUCTION

The chapters in this volume are a series of meditations over the last four decades as the country has evolved and offered opportunities—an arguable and often refuted claim, but while I would accept various caveats, I believe it to be largely true. Much has changed since I arrived. Currently "diversity" has become a keyword in our society, sometimes even an opportunistic bandwagon, and to achieve equality it appears that everyone must wear a label declaring their race, religion, or skin shade. Of Gujarati Indian descent, I was born in Kenya and raised in Tanzania in a small, devotional community. I experienced both colonialism and these two African nations' freedom. My background straddles cultures, religions, and nationalities; therefore when stuck with a label (or put inside a box as I sometimes imagine) I tend to squirm. While acceptance of difference is desirable, indeed essential, I believe that too rigid an adherence to this concept, too inflexible our idea of identity raises a disturbing question. Do we now live divided into separate entities, suspicious of each other, catering only to our racial or tribal selves, or do we accept differences as components of a common citizenship and humanity—your history is mine, your stories mine, your imagination mine?

1

Nowhere Anywhere

1. Nowhere in the World

My mother was born in 1920, in British-protected Zanzibar, of parents who had emigrated from the state of Gujarat in western India. When she was still a girl her family moved to Mombasa. At nineteen she was married to a man from Nairobi; some thirteen years later when our father died suddenly, and the Mau Mau freedom struggle was at its peak, she moved with us, her children, to Dar es Salaam where her family had moved meanwhile. Fifteen years later, having run a small shop and then a small business from home, she returned to Nairobi, where she had been perhaps the happiest. Later still she hustled to Syracuse, New York, with my younger brother where he did a medical internship, and thence she moved with him to Calgary. She spent her last days unhappily in a Toronto nursing home, confined to a wheelchair, maintaining that she was in a prison, a *kaid khano*. Often she would declare her wish to return to Calgary, where she thought she had been happier; and sometimes she protested, "Send me to Nairobi" or "I can live by myself in Dar es Salaam."

Where, then, did she belong? The answer, I believe—using a concept that came to me gradually and reluctantly over the years—is, nowhere in particular. Home was this one, and also that one; this one in one context, and that one in another; this one today, that one tomorrow. Visiting her, I would wonder, Where is she today, where does she want to go? Often I would be reminded of Sir Percy, hero of *The Scarlet Pimpernel* (1905), of whom it was said, "We seek him here, we seek him there / ... Is he in heaven? Is he in hell?"[1] Not surprisingly, Baroness Orczy, creator of this flitting, elusive character, was herself an immigrant. In this condition, home is never a single place, entirely and unequivocally. It is contingent. The abstract "Nowhere," then, is the true home.

I come from an itinerant community traditionally known as the Khojas, originating loosely across the areas of western India abutting the Arabian Sea, known as Kathiawad and Kutch in the present-day state of Gujarat. For centuries, people from that region have been known to set off across the seas as traders and settlers, east to Ceylon (Sri Lanka), Burma (Myanmar), and further, or west and south across the Indian Ocean as far as Oman, Mombasa, Kilwa, and Zanzibar. It is to this inherent, itinerant tendency that I attribute my own family's somewhat nomadic existence. I went to university to the United States at the age of twenty and after eight years, spent first in Cambridge, Massachusetts and later in Philadelphia, I proceeded for my postdoctoral work to Deep River, Ontario (population 5500), and two years later to Toronto. The move to Philadelphia was unnecessary, but I needed to get away. When finally with a young family

I landed in a house in North Toronto, after a stint downtown, it was with a sinking feeling and the thought: Am I stuck here? For how long? After four decades now (travelling as an author having provided much release to my vagrant spirit) Toronto is, practically, home. It is a place where, after my travels, I have returned to my family. I have a stake in its quality and its future. I appreciate its many services, and like all Torontonians I have my gripes about them. I have contributed to its life. It matters to me. And yet there is that home from where memory and history beckon, from where the old sights and sounds echo unprompted, at times with a sentimental stab. It is the place from where the muse calls with inspiration: people and places remembered, nuances unexplored. In the best of cases, history finally comes along and segues into the recent past which has become new history; or it stays behind and leaves a hole in the consciousness as life moves on. The muse too may come along bearing the wounds of departure; or like a disappointed genie simply vanish.

I have at times been assailed by a deep sense of nostalgia—not the pink-tinged one of longing for the idealized good times of the past; we all have those and dismiss them for what they are, brief and often joyful respites from the travails of daily life. My childhood with a widowed mother raising five children had many happy moments of togetherness, but there were also the painful ones of struggle. What I have in mind by nostalgia is my deep envy of those people who casually display a fulsome sense of their identity and place in the world. They belong completely to a place, are one with its soil—its language and rhythms, its songs and stories, its hills and valleys, and the gods who wandered on that landscape. As a student in Boston I was witness to the media fanfare that accompanied the Russian author Alexander Solzhenitsyn's arrival in the United States. He was cheered and honoured in the US, but he had been forced into exile. Two decades later when the Soviet Union collapsed, he returned to Russia and eventually died there. There never seemed to have been any doubt in him where his real home was. All his novels were passionately about Mother Russia, written in his native language. What a sense of belonging and home! To be of a place, a landscape and its seasons, a culture, a history and language. This sense of belonging was displayed to me in a different way in India once, as I watched a new acquaintance casually go to a small shrine in her home and do a salutation to the idol before departing. It was the most natural, simple, habitual gesture of someone at home in a place where her family had lived forever, praying to gods identified with the mountains and rivers and temples, who've been there forever too, and whose fantastic and magical deeds across the land are everyone's stories. This sense of the land as a part of your being is often captured beautifully in the poignant words of Canada's Indigenous poets. The Innu poet Joséphine Bacon says, "Your heart heard the land."[2]

    The Indigenous have been denied rights and faced brutal discrimination and abuse in the land to which they belong more truly than any other people. Their nostalgia is for where they are right now; they have not gone away, their home has moved away. Over several centuries they have seen diverse populations arrive and be given the right to stay and grow, become proud, patriotic

Canadians, while more and more they, the Aboriginal peoples, are marginalized. India too has its Indigenous people—the Adivasis ("first residents"), who survive on the fringes—as do many other countries that were occupied or colonized. India's cruel caste system adds another feature of rejection of a people in their own land. Due to the Partition of South Asia, which created Muslim-majority independent Pakistan, the Muslims of independent India often find themselves in the precarious position of having their loyalty challenged. The taunt "Go to Pakistan!" is often heard during times of communal strife. Where, they ask, do they belong, when their ethnic roots in the land go back centuries and even millennia?[3] The Asians of East Africa have similarly found their loyalty questioned by the majority. Where do they belong? they've often had to ask themselves. I am reminded of a friend of mine, an Asian African, who, during a street vendors' grievance against Asian businesses in Dar es Salaam, Tanzania, was taunted in the street by a Black African, "Go back to Bombay!" To which she replied instantly, "Your father will go to Bombay!" which sounds sharper in Swahili and Gujarati: *Babako ataenda Bombay*; *Taro baap jaashe Mumbai*. She was going nowhere. Her response was of someone who belongs, even when challenged.

Is the contrary condition that I describe for myself, then, my inability to feel completely and uniquely of a place, because different loyalties claim me—causing me embarrassment and tying me up in a web of contradictions (and, perhaps, lies)—a defect of character or mind? If only there were a cure, a procedure to enable one simply to draw oneself in, tortoise-like, away from those memories and ties of elsewhere, to cut off those links that feed us and yet destabilize us with delusions and inflict upon us the aches of loss, nostalgia, and envy. Trying to imagine a situation in which one could artificially rid oneself of one's past and begin life anew, in a state of dejection I came upon the inspiration for my novel *Nostalgia*. What if there existed a surgical or chemical process by which memory could be erased and replaced with a new one? Nostalgia in my novel is defined by the condition in which the past leaks in small quantities into the present and keeps growing, creating havoc in the mind—until a specialist mends the leak. The novel, then, is an ironic look at the idea of assimilation. There can never be total assimilation; the past remains.

Immigrants upon first arrival, with relief at their success after a trying and often humiliating application process, and perhaps with bitterness and anger at what drove them away, can well claim, "I am a Canadian now," and add con brio, "Forget the past!" Despite this bravado, they walk around with a wound—from broken lives, broken careers and ambitions—as they start afresh, learning new ways while exulting in the new comforts, but always existing at a slant from the native-born white. They bring along their cultures and languages, their foods and festivals, their social circles, their quarrels and prejudices that are not easily forgotten. In their new country they are easily identified as alien, a "minority," betrayed by their features, their speech, their manners, their gaffes. (A man from Tanzania whom I knew would get up and offer his seat to any white woman who got on the bus, to the utter humiliation of his family.) The immigrants are given new labels they never imagined before; they become statistics, treated as victims, are anything but normal people. The onslaught of memories soon begins; memories that have to be tamed and given a place in their renewed lives. Going away is a slow process, hardly ever completed.

Some memories are undoubtedly pathological. In the novel *The Thin Line* by Albanian Canadian Perparim Kapllani,[4] a boy grows up, having witnessed the massacre of his family by neighbours during the Bosnian war in the 1990s, with one principal objective: to return to his hometown with an automatic rifle and exact revenge. Similarly in Nur Abdi's novel *The Somali Camel Boy*,[5] a former simpleton camel-herder arrives in Toronto with the objective of exacting revenge on any member of the enemy tribe whose members had killed his father.

Sheniz Janmohamed, a poet born in Ontario of Kenyan Asian parents, illustrates how the process of going away is never completed, even after generations following removal from the homeland. In the introduction to her third book of poetry, *Reminders on the Path*,[6] she informs us that her work "is rooted in the language of nature and place, from the desert terrain of Kutch [India] to the Rift Valley in Kenya to the deciduous forests of Turtle Island [Canada]." Growing up different in white surroundings, she had felt that she did not belong anywhere, until she visited her ancestral homeland, Kenya, and made connection with her grandmother, and followed up this reconnection by visiting her other homeland, India, eventually learning to see her life as the continuation of a series of journeys, hers and her ancestors'. Here again one hears an echo from Joséphine Bacon: "a song / freezes in your memory // you become the ancestor / of your ancestors."[7]

For the Indigenous American (in the larger, continental sense), in contrast, as for someone like the once-exiled Alexander Solzhenitsyn of my college days or my Indian friend, home is that unique place that speaks to the heart. You could be denied that home; but you could still claim to belong to it. Your belonging to a place cannot be defined by those who currently happen to rule over it.

There is a difference between identity and belonging, which are often confused. Identity is a description, it is what you tick off in today's official forms declaring your particulars: South Asian, Indo-Canadian, Black Canadian, LGBTQ, etc. If you are the right kind, there may be government benefits in the spirit of restitutions. You may claim an Indian or African identity without having been to those places, or even being able to survive there. Belonging, on the other hand, is what Joséphine Bacon refers to. It's that unequivocal, sentimental call of the land to the heart. It's what makes you recall the smell of the air, with the first breath you take outside the airport when you return.

The Asian immigrants who came from Tanzania in the 1970s loudly proclaimed themselves Canadians, believing firmly they had left Africa behind. And yet they went about recreating in Don Mills, Ontario precisely the character of the neighbourhoods they had left behind, around the prayer and social hall, the jamat khana, which was at first a room in a shopping mall or a school gym; their apartments were within walking distance of that centre, and their groceries and foods, hairdressers, insurance agents, etc. were all dispersed around the neighbourhood. Had they left their Dar es Salaam far behind? It would take time for that to happen, and even then, not completely. Many from their children's generation, having grown up or been born in Canada, following family rootlessness and migratory traditions, were setting off to other countries for their higher education and choosing eventually to serve—as Canadians—anywhere in the world, including their parents' Africa. Distance seems to mean nothing.

It does not seem unusual or shocking for me to hear from those taking stock of their lives, after some forty years in Canada, a statement like, I don't feel at home anywhere, where can I possibly retire? Canada still seems safest, but they feel they just don't completely belong. (This feeling is partly due, of course, to the anxiety of aging; older people are exiles everywhere, but you can choose, wealth permitting, to be exiled in a warmer place that is also familiar.)

2. Nowhere in Canada

In Toronto, I draw comfort from the presence of people like me who all have a qualifier to their Canadian-ness; who are still possessed by other places. This is a modern condition; few in Canada or America, except the Indigenous, can say, We've always lived on this land, our roots here go back to the hoary past. At my gym, called the Columbus Centre, many people speak Italian, fluently or in interjections, and there is a baritone who throws out his chest and sings a popular aria as he arrives to do his bicycle routine. Italian achievements, such as victories in World Cup soccer, are celebrated with congratulatory posters. People of Irish origin have a special attachment to Ireland. People of Indian origin—the so-called NRIs—as well as Portuguese Canadians and others often buy retirement homes in their native or ancestral countries. The Indian government gives the NRIs a special status and identity paper, and they celebrate India's Independence Day annually in Toronto at a function where they sing with due gusto both the Canadian and the Indian anthems, dignitaries from both countries in attendance.

As long as there is movement from place to place, so long as people emigrate from nation to nation, from one culture to another, there will always be those in transition, who live in several places—or nowhere completely. They will grow genuinely fond of their host countries, to which they will make their contributions in various forms and to various degrees. But they will continue to live in a state of tension: the laws of their new homes confer upon them rights of belonging and citizenship they might not have enjoyed before; they have become used to the comforts and efficiencies of their new countries, where they have grown roots; but they also feel a sense of belonging to their native countries and cultures. Childhood doesn't let go overnight. Even for later generations, as Sheniz Janmohamed illustrates, a visit to the ancestral homeland is an essential ritual for many young people to feel at home with themselves.

The problem arises when there comes a conflict between the different places of one's claim, as it did during the two great wars of the twentieth century. During World War I, suddenly German and Austrian Canadians became targets of hostility and surveillance. Thousands were interned, others had to register, and humiliating caricatures of their race were a commonplace ("Once a German, Always a German"). A similar fate awaited the Japanese Canadians during the Second World War. This latter case has received more attention because it is recent and has been acknowledged as a shameful episode in the nation's history. It has been poignantly recounted in works of literature, such as Joy Kogawa's novel *Obasan*.[8]

One may well ask, a question rarely asked, Is it fair to expect such conflicted populations to turn on hatred suddenly, on demand as it were, and reject those places that contain beloved childhood memories and familial, ancestral, religious, and cultural ties? Some young people will do so, in the proverbial battle of generations, son against father, immigrants' offspring against parents' origins. Though, as we know, in time the child looks into the mirror and sees the parent staring back. Thus, during WWI many young Canadians of German and Austrian origin queued up to go to Europe to fight for the Central Powers. Others made the cut with their ancestry cleanly and enlisted in the Canadian army—though they would still have faced discrimination and suspicion.

One evening, while at a meeting in a college town in the United States, when a similar question came up, I asked an Indian American engineer explicitly, if India and America came into conflict, which side would he support. Without hesitation, he said: India. But it's not so simple, as he must surely have known. He was enjoying the benefits of living affluently in his adopted country, and his children were growing up Americans first.

In both the world wars Canada was not specifically attacked; it lay far away across the Atlantic and there was no threat to its land mass. But the British Empire was at war, of which Canada was an integral part—"Britain's loyal daughter," as a website of Canadian military history quaintly puts it.[9] Few would argue that if Canada itself had come under attack, citizens of all backgrounds would have fought to defend it.

But then—to ask a question recently gaining prominence—was it, or is it their land in the first place? More and more is it acknowledged that the land belongs to those who were living here before the Europeans came. Boilerplate statements dutifully proclaim at every public event that every day we stand and sit on grounds originally belonging to an Indigenous nation. (Though, as overheard in an auditorium, "If they tell us to go, where will we go?") No matter how robotic and irrelevant such proclamations may sound in a lecture hall, there can be little doubt, and it is increasingly recognized, that the non-Indigenous races of Canada are merely settlers in a colonized land, just as the Boers of South Africa were.

I have expressed my sense of guilt and betrayal at not being able to be entirely Canadian—someone who can say, I belong nowhere else. But it seems that the country to which I arrived has itself slipped away! It is no longer what it was, or had promoted itself to be. What then is a Canadian, what does it mean to belong to this land? Some of the country's proud symbols seem dated or repugnant. The British Empire is no more, its reminder an embarrassment even in London; the Constitution has been repatriated, the flag is no longer the Union Jack that many of the older people remember saluting. (Though it still occupies a prominent place on several provincial flags, and many place names across the country—from Victoria, British Columbia to Prince Edward Island, from Dufferin to Dundas Streets—hark back to the glory of the British Empire. Even at the national level, the past does not let go so easily.) There are increasing calls for abolishing the British monarchy in Canada.

In September 1916, at the height of WWI, the town of Berlin, Ontario changed its name to Kitchener, to honour the general who in 1898 led the British campaign of conquest in Sudan. He became a hero and was highly decorated. Today we know that his role was not as heroic as has been supposed. Kitchener came to Sudan from Egypt with a small but well-trained professional army, and was engaged by a large force of the followers of a charismatic religious leader called the Mahdi, in what is known as the Battle of Omdurman. The Mahdists were armed with primitive rifles and clumsy muskets; the British came with the most advanced Maxim rifles, faster to load and with a much longer range, plus artillery and a flotilla of gunboats on the Nile. In what has been called "an execution not a battle," wave after wave of the Sudanese were swiftly and casually cut down.[10] Within a few hours the Mahdist force had been destroyed, losing twelve thousand men against Kitchener's forty-seven. Many of the wounded were subsequently executed, for which

Kitchener was criticized. Winston Churchill was an observer of that encounter and wrote about it, not hiding his admiration for the Mahdi's men. His own reputation, however, has also been tarnished recently, especially among South Asians, for his role in the Bengal famine of 1943 and for his well-known racism.

Being a Canadian then is, besides everything else, also to bear the burden of its history of colonization and racism; more than that, it is to accept the fact that the modern nation was built on a foundation of broken treaties and cultural genocide against a population that already thrived on this land. It is not an easy situation.

2

Voices in the Wilderness: The Nowhere Artist

In this nowhere space, this limbo of existence, a special and lingering torment is reserved for the creative artist—the writer, the musician, the painter, the sculptor. How to find acceptance, audience, understanding? An ear to listen? How to establish an artistic presence in this new setting? How to go on living, when living is to do art? Many a painter and sculptor, dancer and musician, poet and story-writer has languished in obscurity or surrendered integrity to peddle patriotic platitudes in order to survive. It's easier to wield the pen when the other hand waves the flag. In desperation, he tries to maintain connections in the home country in order to gain recognition there if nowhere else, but how long can this tenuous thread survive before it frays into nothing?

The tragic fate of Trishanku, a character in Indian mythology, gives us an apt illustration of this nowhere existence. Trishanku was the name given to King Satyavrata of the solar dynasty, an ancestor of the hero Rama of the epic *Ramayana*. He was a righteous king, the Sanskritic *Satyavrata* implies, but caught by a fit of vanity one day he told himself he should by rights belong to the heavenly pantheon among the gods. The powerful sage Vishwamitra came to his aid and fulfilled his wish by performing the required rites, but when the king arrived in heaven, the god Indra, playing the gatekeeper many of us have met at various national borders, hurled him back. Tumbling down to earth, he was caught midair by the sage, who assigned him then to a special corner of the universe, where he now hangs suspended upside down, neither here nor there. Trishanku can be seen as a cluster of stars in the constellation of the Southern Cross.

Trishanku gives the name to a long poem (or cycle of poems) by Uma Parameswaran of Manitoba, in which she explores the poignant theme of "wanting to belong" as it applies to immigrants in Canada in the 1970s and 80s. Parameswaran is a poet, dramatist, and novelist, and much of her work of that period, including the play *Rootless But Green Are the Boulevard Trees*, touch upon this theme.[1]

I met the painter and sculptor Youngo—his full name, I would later learn, was Youngo Verma—at an exhibition of his works at the Goethe Institute in Toronto, to which I was taken by M. H. K. Qureshi, the Urdu editor of the literary magazine *The Toronto South Asian Review (TSAR)*, which I had recently co-founded. It was 1981. Even to a non-expert like me, the startling originality and intensity of Youngo's sculptures and drawings was evident, as was his utter seriousness and dedication. A shortish, stocky man with a pointed goatee and the distant gaze of the visionary, he spoke in a somewhat disinterested, dry voice that made one wonder if he was really all there.

Unlike other South Asian artists of that period, whose works were charming abstract sketches in colour (already an indication of rootlessness), Youngo's work was meticulously detailed, involving semi-representational forms such as a metal camera as the human eye, or drawings of smooth shapes evoking sensual and mystical energy. He had received his early training in the Delhi College of Art. Influenced by the Bauhaus style and inspired particularly by the Romanian modernist Constantin Brancusi, he set off for Frankfurt, Germany to study sculpture at the prestigious Städelschule. Ten years later he came to Canada. What brought him away from his sources of influence remains a mystery. But for the three and a half decades he spent in Toronto until his death, he worked in isolation and poverty, producing a large number of works. He lived in Mississauga in a one-bedroom townhouse that was his studio, cluttered so much with his works that there was little room to walk through. He had a few admirers in the Indo-Pakistani community, but his one close friend and constant support was the gallery owner Ali Adil Khan, who curated three exhibitions for him. Says Adil Khan, "I used to visit him almost every week to check on him. When he was ill, I used to take soup and food for him as he had no one to look after him. Also, on his annual visit to India, he would ask me to drop him at the airport, and carry his luggage to the counter, which I happily did. He loved biryani and red wine and I would often pick it up for him."

Did he really belong anywhere—influenced both by Indian and European traditions, residing penuriously in Canada, unrecognized? Winters he spent in India for some years but stopped visiting after he was cheated of some ancestral property by a relative. He watched with envy as artists of his generation in India became wealthy and celebrated, among whom he no longer belonged. In Canada he succumbed to temptation a couple of times to apply for high-profile public commissions that were clearly beneath his talent, futile attempts at recognition, and predictably failed. He died in 2014, leaving some four hundred works in his estate, thirty of which were accepted as a gift by the Royal Ontario Museum in Toronto. The Art Gallery of Mississauga put up an exhibition of his work, but with a qualifier: an artist of the "diaspora." An outsider.[2]

Peng Ma from China is another example of a full-fledged talent floundering on the shores of the Canadian arts scene. He had already received recognition in Mao's China, where he had also taught at a university. Brush painting has a long tradition in China and involves an artist's interpretation of a real scene, such as a landscape. To Peng Ma, Western abstraction presented an intellectual and artistic challenge. He came to Canada in the 1980s among the small tide of Chinese immigrants that began arriving in the West. An obsessive worker, calling himself an experimental traditionalist—"Tradition is my root"—he produced numerous Canadian landscapes as well as abstractions in ink. His local promoter worked tirelessly to find him exhibition space, producing a catalogue to introduce him to Canada. He could not penetrate the mainstream. Recognition came in his native China, where he visited regularly and received commissions, and from the Chinese immigrant community of Canada. In her story "Under the Big Tree,"[3] scholar and writer Lien Chao presents a vivid contrast between the artists who remained in China and became famous and wealthy in the new and booming consumer economy and those struggling to find a voice in Canada.

In the West we often perceive artists as eccentric radicals existing outside the mainstream and the mundane. If lucky, they progress from obscurity to fame and become household names and legends. Andy Warhol and Lucien Freud come readily to mind. And yet artistic traditions are long and conservative, deeply rooted, of which modern artists are well aware and to which they are reacting, as each new generation does towards the previous one. How does a sculptor or painter, born in India, Africa, or China fit into the Canadian mainstream art culture? As the art critic Deepali Dewan says of P. Mansaram, another artist from India, "... the conservative collecting environment in Canada, long geared toward landscape painting, had little room for his art. There was also the added burden of being a brown man in a white space that gave visibility to only certain forms of creativity."[4]

Youngo died a lonely artist, P. Mansaram with a sense of failure, while Peng Ma in his senior years continues to work energetically at the margins of Canadian art.

Similarly, a vocalist or dancer trained classically in a South Asian tradition since childhood finds appreciation only in immigrant suburbs such as those of Toronto and Vancouver. Attempts at creating original-themed classical dances such as Bharat Natyam in Canada may seem like planting seeds in hostile terrain. With new generations trained locally, they may well in due time develop into the legitimately authentic. Meanwhile performers from the source—South Asia—still have the power to draw large South Asian audiences. The finest dancers and vocalists have been brought from India and Pakistan and have found enthusiastic audiences in Canada, albeit usually at a suburban hall or the home of a wealthy patron. Still, dance and singing, being obviously evocative with music and exotic costumery, can draw some "downtown" audiences, even if they have to travel to the burbs.

One may well ask, why go away in the first place, away from the muse and into a blank space? The answers are many. Sometimes it is a young person, seduced by media hype, chasing the illusion of financial security and artistic glory in the West, or it's simply an escape from the hustle of a crowded space governed by mind-numbing bullying and corrupt bureaucracy, or it's exile from war or repression. Writers often arrive from non-Western countries with fantastic ideas about the book market, expecting instant publication and a ready readership. I have met writers brought to Canada by well-meaning charities and given a residency for a year or two, after which in this impersonal culture they are left to languish in that limbo to do the best they can. Rarely do they get the renown or appreciation they enjoyed in their home countries.

Some wonderful, indeed great Tamil literature is produced in Canada, its inspiration often fed by the trauma and grief of the Sri Lankan civil war, which resulted in some hundreds of thousands ending up in exile across the globe and a tragic aftermath at home that has been described as a war crime. The Toronto novelist Devakanthan's magnificent quintet of novels,

Prison of Dreams,[5] describes the evolution of this tragedy, beginning with new Sinhalese-nationalist laws of the island that marginalized the Tamil minority of mostly Dravidian Hindus and a smaller number of Muslims. (The Sinhalese majority are Buddhist and related, linguistically at least, to northern India.) In Devakanthan's quintet, the rising resentment of Tamil youth and their disenchantment with Gandhian non-violence as a means of protest leads to armed resistance and dreams of a separate Tamil homeland, and finally and inevitably to catastrophe. Much of Sri Lankan Tamil writing comes from Toronto, which has a large exile community.

At the other, western end of the country in British Columbia, Punjabi writing has thrived for decades. The Punjabis have lived in the province for more than a century, and their literature—poetry, fiction, and drama—deals with themes of exile and social issues within the community. A Japanese ship, the *Komagata Maru*, has become the focus of the founding myth of Punjabi Sikh presence in Canada. One day in May 1914 the *Komagata Maru* arrived in Vancouver harbour from British Hong Kong bearing 376 Punjabi prospective immigrants, a majority of them Sikhs. In 1908, Canada's Parliament had added the perverse "continuous journey" amendment to the Immigration Act of 1906, requiring immigrants to arrive on these shores directly from their country of birth. Due to this obstacle, very obviously designed to keep Asian immigrants away, and the obstinacy of a single official displaying the doggedness of Victor Hugo's Inspector Javert, only twenty-four passengers of the *Komagata Maru* were admitted into the country and the ship was escorted ignominiously out of Vancouver harbour by a Canadian naval vessel. Arriving in Calcutta it was met by the police, and a riot ensued in which at least twenty people died.

The *Komagata Maru* incident has given Punjabi writers a potent symbol—of their identity and struggles and their claim to Canada—though perhaps it has been excessively flogged as a subject of poems, books, plays, and films.[6] Generational conflict has also been explored in Canada's Punjabi writing, for example by the poet and story writer Sadhu Binning,[7] who also touches on the relationships of the early Punjabi farm workers, single men, with local Indigenous women.

Relevant, good, and sometimes great as this writing in the vernacular is, it belongs to its community—the Tamil, the Punjabi, the Hindi, the Urdu, the Mandarin. Translations are made, but the circulation in English remains small, in the few hundreds. The loneliness and despair of these writers is profound, as witnesses Surjeet Kalsey in her poem "Siddhartha Does Penance Once Again,"[8] comparing the departure of the immigrant from Punjab to the departure of the Buddha (Siddhartha) from his family; but the nirvana the immigrant finds, after a long day's work in the berry fields of British Columbia, is his bottle of alcohol. And finally, says this immigrant, "an artist within me has died / I've become one of the dumbly driven cattle."

To add to his despair, the persevering writer is well aware that he is not germinating or propagating a tradition: the new generations, born in Canada, are versed only in English. The only recourse for acknowledgement, encouragement, and inspiration is to look out to the world—the lovers of literature everywhere

where the "diaspora" has spread. The "Nowhere" space of the literary artist then spreads out, literary and linguistic identity distills from the identity of mere citizenship. The Dhahan Prize for Punjabi Literature, founded in Vancouver, knows no borders.[9]

The writer in English sees greater hope of building a bridge from his Trishanku limbo-land to that heaven where literary glory apparently resides, where he can be read and understood by a large audience, at least in principle. But it's a narrow bridge to cross. Not every writer from what used aptly—honestly—to be called "the third world" captures the interest of the mainstream; even in English, he may not conform to the current Euro-American styles of expression; or he is much too foreign. He brings idiom, history, ethos and aesthetic that traditional editors are not equipped for and therefore quick to dismiss his work as unmarketable.

Today the fashion in the West (the "first world") may be Black; previously it was India. Some years ago when I had gone to sign at a bookstore in London, England, the owner made to me what seemed to him an encouraging comment that since my novel was about Indians in Africa (and presumably not Africans in Africa), it was more saleable. In these different times now, publishers are quick to snap up young Black writers raised in Canada in the name of diversity; they share a culture ("Canadian") with the younger generation, who are moreover savvy with social media and eager to promote their own works.

But there is little understanding or empathy for writers actually from and writing about Africa. Quebec is better in this respect, especially with regard to francophone Africa.

The world that feeds the immigrant marginal's memory and creative impulse is not simply the country they have left behind, but its involvement with the large "third" world with its manyfold issues. It's impossible not to see the interconnectedness of countries that make up this admittedly loose entity. (The term "non-aligned" described most of these countries previously.) Writers from South Asia, the Caribbean, and East and West Africa know the common language of exile, indenture, colonialism, and racism. When I meet a taxi driver from Pakistan or Somalia, there is an understanding between us (the Somali might speak some Swahili and have come as an exile via Nairobi, my birthplace); immigrants from Africa and the Caribbean bear the history of colonialism and slavery. All now speak the language of marginalization and neglect.

Dannabang Kuwabong, a Canadian poet from Ghana and professor of English in Puerto Rico, finds his Africanness resonate in the Caribbean via memories of the Atlantic slave trade:

> I look down from on high the B767
> catch glimpses of ghosts of ancient ships
> retching their black human cargo
> upon this salt-saturated soil[10]

(Wole Soyinka, Nigerian Nobel laureate partly resident in the United States, writes in his memoirs of visiting a village in Brazil that carried memories of its roots among his people, the Yoruba, and finding disappearing remnants of his culture in a settlement in Jamaica.[11])

The immigrant or exile from that other world is haunted by it. But more and more it doesn't know him—a new generation has arrived, the political system may have changed, the conversations are different, there is a new vocabulary in town. And he himself is no longer the same. His habits of mind and body are different; he has family constraints—the roots he has planted in his new country have sunk deeper; he cannot merely pack up and go away. He is caught in-between, like Trishanku. To whom and for whom should he write? To what purpose? Is anyone listening? A lone prophet, he must write. Like a pioneer ventured out on an uncultivated land, he starts digging and building, he unloads. His baggage is stuffed with the stories and histories of his native land, its poetry and mythology, and even its concerns in the world, its own struggles to belong. If he has the strength to feed his inspiration, and the will to pick up the pen or the laptop, he writes, and writes. Trapped in his limbo-land, alternately facing up and facing down, north and south, he shouts his stories to both the worlds.

If she is not a mere hustler, she tries to remain true to her inspiration, to the stories and thoughts she has brought that clamour to come out. But how does she describe her alien characters, convey the pulse of another place, the rhythm of another language, other mythologies and idioms to her new prospective audience? A shadow of "second-class" and irrelevance looms over every endeavour. Labels like "multicultural," "alien," "ethnic," and "diverse" are thrown at her, not simply "artist." As the novelist H. Nigel Thomas says,

> Astonishing how, regardless of what we accomplish in our adopted country, every aspect of our being remains circumscribed by race or ethnicity. At best I can be called a multicultural writer. My ontology is a blend of British colonial education, Afro-Caribbean rituals and folkways, fifty-plus years of living and studying in Canada (some of it in the heartland of French Canada, Quebec City), and a gay sensibility.[12]

These artists belong to their separate heaven, a small space in which well-wishers and admirers can see, read, and hear their work. Thomas, like Kuwabong, is published by small, dedicated presses. The world of established publishers, galleries, theatres, and organizations has continuously closed their doors to them; but regardless, they demonstrate a fanatical, obsessive resilience of the artistic impulse, a militancy: to create, "in spite of," and as they must; they are a continuing protest for relevance and belonging, for they have arrived, after all, to a democracy, however flawed.

Perhaps, with the new, emerging attitudes to the concept of identity, when "diversity" is the rage, the changes that have occurred are real and not superficial. But more of that in a later chapter.

Six years after coming to Canada, Rahul Varma co-founded a dramatic company called Teesri Duniya Theatre in Montreal, a city where cultural activity thrives. (The term *teesri duniya* means "third world.") Yet his career has been one of rejection, struggle, and confrontation. With titles such as *Job-Stealer* (referring to the immigrant), *Equal Wages*, and *Isolated Incident* (about the shooting of an unarmed Black man in Montreal) his works take on urgent domestic issues; the other half of his literary persona has dealt with global themes, such as the American invasion of Iraq, the Rwandan genocide, and the Union Carbide tragedy in Bhopal, India, in a bid to bring the world into Canada. As he says,

> I have an impressive record of failure of winning support as a writer and as an Artistic Director of Teesri Duniya Theatre in my home province. But I also have an impressive history of writing and producing diverse plays despite lack of patronage.[13]

Varma has achieved grudging acceptance as a Quebec playwright, but only in a backhanded way as the wonderful, multicultural Other who reflects the diversity of this great country. But surely, as soon as a label is put on an artist that is not put on others generally, he has been dispatched to that other side, the universe of the upstarts.

When I arrived in Cambridge, Massachusetts as an undergraduate student, I was greeted by a wonderland of bookstores. We had decent ones in my childhood in Dar es Salaam, though catering mostly to expatriate tastes. In any case, few of us locals could afford to purchase books. The most you could do was to browse hungrily at them in display windows, or if they were Agatha Christie or Enid Blyton, try to read a few pages at a time on a bookshelf, the owner watching suspiciously before coming over to tell you to scram. There were a small number of libraries in town, including our school library with an antique collection (Billy Bunter, Beagles) and the British Council library in the leafy European area and unapproachable by the likes of me. The Ismaili community library was my real introduction to the world of books. It had books in Gujarati and English, and a reading room containing British comics like *The Beano* and *The Dandy*, among other offerings. It was a thrill to stroll through its hallowed aisles, to browse and actually take a book home to read. ("Really? I can take it home?" "Yes, and bring it back in a few days.") When I was older, I discovered the town's public library with its richer treasure.

Books were an escape from chores and well-meaning cheek-pulling relatives who could just drop in for a visit. They were my window to different worlds, real and fantastic, with different people and their stories, told in different ways. One of my most memorable discoveries, there in distant Dar es Salaam, was James Baldwin's *Another Country*. It had a profound effect on me though also left me mystified: the world out there was far and alien. I recall writing a class essay on it, which a teacher, fresh from America, read aloud. Sometimes I would wish for books set *here*, in Dar, in Uhuru Street or Upanga, about people like me. Now in Cambridge I found bookstores galore and I discovered many books and authors as a student, among them Heinrich Böll, Günter Grass, Witold Gombrowicz, Hermann Hesse, Tolstoy, Dostoevsky, Freud and Jung and many others. I could connect with the world of these disparate authors, but there was hardly anything by an African or a South Asian, and this began to matter more to me as a young person away from home, because I realized that I was not represented in this wonderful cornucopia of literature. What if...?

And so finally, addressing this deficit in our reading experiences, which began to irk more and more, soon after our arrival in Toronto some years later, in the heat of an excited discussion a few of us decided to take the issue head-on and start a literary magazine of our own, which we called *The Toronto South Asian Review*. (This venture, in retrospect, sometimes seems to have been foolhardy, because it took so much work and sacrifice, but I have spared another place and time to describe its history.) The name was obviously too restrictive, for we had all come from East Africa, and so the magazine soon became *The Toronto Review of Contemporary Writing Abroad*. Through it we went on to discover and learn much from writers from former colonies of the British Empire who had for one reason or another washed up on different shores, many currently residing in the cosmopolitan centres and college towns of North America but others in its far corners, who grasped at our magazine (or journal, as we also called it) like castaways on a desert clutching at a small camel-load of water that has just arrived.

There was no other journal like it. Muhammad Umar Memon from Wisconsin translated Urdu stories into English; Reshard Gool from Prince Edward Island wrote about the infamous evacuation of non-whites from Cape Town's District Six in Apartheid South Africa; Himani Bannerji re-evaluated a popular Bengali novelist; Yvonne Vera wrote stories set in post-independence Zimbabwe; Marlene Nourbese Philip reviewed the Canadian novelist Arnold Itwaru's Guyanese tragedy *Shanti*; Arun Prabha Mukherjee did a review of South Asian poetry in Canada; Frank Birbalsingh introduced Indo-Caribbean writing; Surjeet Kalsey wrote stories about the lives of Punjabi women in British Columbia. We published anthologies, the kind never published anywhere before—Sri Lankan writing, Punjabi writing, Indo-Caribbean writing. And so a brave new world of literature opened up for me and others, separate from—or in opposition to—the American-British-Canadian mainstream. The poetry, fiction, and criticism we published described experiences, thoughts, and feelings that resonated with readers and writers from diverse regions of the globe who seemed to share a certain identity and view of the world. The gods of English Literature, such as Northrop Frye and Harold Bloom, might not have allowed it into their world, but it was here, it was vibrant and organic, and it was to stay. It would be a long time before writers from such diverse backgrounds would be accepted as legitimately Canadian. But how deep this recognition goes, how it discerns, and how much of it is mere tokenism remains to be seen. (At present we seem to have arrived at the "reparations" stage.) The magazine, at a hundred pages an issue and three issues a year, lasted twenty years, making up some six thousand pages in total, and gave rise to the publishing company Mawenzi House, which continued the same work but with books.

At about the same time as our magazine was founded, the Toronto International Festival of Authors (TIFA) started. It brought many renowned authors to our city, including Salman Rushdie and Ted Hughes. Meanwhile at the other end of town Urdu literary groups were bringing to the city some of the biggest names of twentieth-century Indo-Pakistani literature, and 150 years of Indian indentureship in the Caribbean were commemorated with a festival and an anthology. In Vancouver, Punjabi plays were drawing audiences in the hundreds. Different festivals, different audiences, far apart.

―――

The subject of "international" festivals requires a small addendum, which I cannot resist, if only for the sake of history.

We, the "other" literary community, had tried repeatedly for over twenty years to convince the program directors of the Toronto International Festival of Authors to take a peek outside their windows at the demographic of Toronto and send out author invitations accordingly; that is, in addition to European, British, and American authors, to include in its programs also authors from Africa and Asia, where many Torontonians have roots. (In North America, "international" or "world" often means "local." Compare the World Series of baseball with the World Cup of soccer.) The festival—then calling itself grandly the International Festival of Authors—had become a powerful entity, internationally renowned, a promoter of literature in Canada; but whose literature? Not surprisingly, the majority of its audiences were white Canadians. Deaf to our pleas and requests, it continued to groom its reputation of "world-class." And it was untouchable. The arrogance of its directors became legendary, and they were treated by Canadian publishers—the local hosts of the international authors—with respect and caution. It was a matter of pride for a director of programming to say, "I sat for dinner with such-and-such [American or British writer]." To have sat down for a meal with Salman! With Ian! With Anne! was a lifetime's achievement for these provincials. If someone from Africa or Asia were invited, they would likely be a visitor or an exile already in the United States. From a business perspective, this attitude was understandable—American and Western European governments were only too happy to support their own writers and promote their cultures abroad; but it was hardly acceptable in Toronto. The last time I had this conversation, somewhat unseemingly heated, admittedly, with a Festival director was when a "Belgian Night" was being contemplated.

And so with a sense of outrage, not a little naivety and, some would say, courage, a few of us decided to organize our own international literary festival, reflecting what *we* meant by "international," beginning with a celebration of the twentieth anniversary of the *Toronto Review*'s founding. The *Review*, because of its founding mandate, had developed a connection with Asian Canadians, many of whom were by this time well heeled and ready with donations; the Canada Council was happy to support, as was my publisher Random House. The main argument we used in our grant applications was the unfairness of TIFA. Our venues, partly donated, were the Munk Centre and rooms at Trinity College, the University of Toronto. And so we brought to our city writers from the Philippines, Zimbabwe, Tanzania, India, Pakistan, Sri Lanka, Bangladesh, and the Caribbean, in addition to some twenty Canadian writers of similar origin, for a three-day festival every two years. Among the visitors were a Muslim writer from Sri Lanka and a Dalit writer from Gujarat, hardly on any mainstream radar but with much to say about the conditions of their discriminated-against communities. Other visitors included Girish Karnad, the great twentieth-century Indian dramatist (on his way home from Yale), Walter Bgoya of Tanzania (a doyen of African publishing), Bapsi Sidhwa, the Pakistani American Parsi writer, and Zulfikar Ghose, from many places but in recent decades from the US. There were qawwali recitals, dance performances, and African percussion, with appropriate food.

It was not easy to bring writers from non-Western countries to Canada—visa applications supported by our invitations would usually fall on deaf ears—a situation many of us knew from personal experience—and we had to resort to assistance from establishment figures: a former Canadian High Commissioner, a former Governor General of Canada, and so on.

These were thrilling events and they brought us a lot of satisfaction and a sense of triumph. The media, however, despite our press releases, paid no attention. The mainstream white public paid no attention. I recall the fourth such festival when, on the opening night an African author looked around the hall and asked, But where are the Canadians? He meant white people.

After four festivals, over eight years, with much reluctance we gave up. We had shown what was needed, what could be done. We knew what more we could do to bring a greater world, one we could identify with, to our doors. But with limited resources and a voluntary staff, it was simply too difficult to keep going. But those festivals have been sorely missed, and there have been many requests for their revival.

3

The Canadian Identity, or Lack Thereof

> *Nani wanaijenga nchi yetu, mama?*
> *Si waamerika, mama, si waamerika!*
> (Who builds our nation, mother?
> Not the Americans, mother, not the Americans!)
>
> Tanzanian National Service song, 1969

Not America

It has been argued that there is something fundamentally lacking about a nation that fails to create a unifying mythology and identity, a distinctive culture, outlook, and sense of itself. Canada, according to this long-standing strain of self-disapprobation, is a prime example. To the world, it is faceless. It is seen, or has long seen itself, as "good" and moderate but without an essential character. Overall it is wishy-washy about itself. Sitting so close to a giant, influential neighbour sharing the same cultural origins does not help. A 2021 headline in the *Globe and Mail* tells the story: "The Olympic jean jacket perfectly captures our never-ending struggle with national identity."[1] At the start of a hockey match a few years ago at an American venue, Canadians watching on television were outraged to see their national flag flown next to the American flag with its maple leaf pointing down. This gaffe made a strong point. Canadian audiences would have watched the Americans at the hockey arena devoutly looking up at their raised flag, hands to their breasts—the powerful and universally familiar image of American identity and mission. Hollywood for its part has spread emblematic stories of American glory and heroic mission worldwide. Americans have no doubts about who they are. In the words of the former president Ronald Reagan, "we've come from every corner of the earth, from every race and every ethnic background, and we've become a new breed in the world—we're Americans..."[2] This is a wonderful, truly enviable statement of the ideal. But how close is it to the reality? Not very, as was sharply demonstrated during the Black Lives Matter protests and the global outrage following the murder of George Floyd by police in 2020. The new breed had one strong and other smaller fractures.

There have always been Americans and Americans. When I went to the United States, naively from Tanzania, fed as a teenager on Hollywood WWII and Cold War movies, Elvis Presley and John Kennedy, and portrayals of the postwar cool, handsome American, I could not tell an Italian from an Irish American. I did not think of my freshman advisor, Professor Goldstein, as Jewish. I was not aware that parts of the Midwest had been settled by Scandinavians with blond hair. I did not understand what the line "The night they drove Old Dixie down," played frequently on the radio then, could possibly mean. It took but a short time for the realization to dawn. I read Faulkner's Mississippi novels and once, for a literature course, a rather moving book titled *The Mind of the South*. I picked up Northeastern prejudices against the South and ridicule for the conservatives who supported the American war in Vietnam. Black consciousness had been on the rise and the Black Panthers were in the news. There was a siege at Wounded Knee in South Dakota, site of the Lakota massacre of the 1870s. Reagan's "American," clearly, was at least part illusion.

In our times, Jewish, Italian, African, Latino, Indigenous, and other origins are proudly asserted in America. No longer do Jews and immigrants feel the need to assume English-sounding names, and the invented African American first names are a poke in the eye at the old Anglo-American dominant culture. Black History Month and Kwanzaa speak of alternative histories, as do "People's" histories of America, such as Howard Zinn's. New national museums and university departments are dedicated to formerly marginalized populations demanding recognition and redress. The popular television series *The Sopranos* was an unabashed assertion of Italian American identity and history (though not in a form many Americans or Canadians would approve of); and in recent years even the Muslim Eid gets at least a nod or a luncheon from the president of the United States. More recently still, there are calls for revising American history, revisiting past glories, tearing down flawed heroes and putting up new ones representing the country's diverse roots and a more diverse and honest history. It is yet to be seen, however, how deep into the population the recent changes will go. Perhaps a revised "new breed" will emerge.

I am already deep into American trends. What of Canada?

Canada, in contrast, when I arrived from the United States on a fellowship at Chalk River, Ontario in August 1979, touted itself, with an official policy of multiculturalism in place, as anti-melting pot, the antithesis. "We are not Americans" was a claim I often heard. "We are a mosaic." In fact, "Not American" seemed to self-define this nation that seemed more insecure to me than the newly independent African country of my boyhood. It was in an identity crisis of its own. The Union Jack on provincial flags and place names referencing British exploits and heroes—Kitchener, Waterloo, Agincourt, Victoria, Prince Edward, Dundas, Elgin, Dufferin—seemed only to confirm English Canada's shaky identity. However, its growing acceptance of, and indeed its more gentle approach to cultural difference were distinctly attractive. In case I get accused in these finger-pointing times of betrayal and selling out, I will quickly admit that there *was* racism, and I suffered my share of slights—the micro and nano aggressions, real and imagined. (Though the imagined have roots in the real.) But there seemed to me a growing acceptance of difference. Cultural, racial, and ethnic diversity were undeniable, there for all to see and experience. More and more immigrants were coming in; Canada needed them.[3] And consequently, Canada was adjusting itself to their presence.

To me the image of a mosaic was disagreeable and threatening: a mosaic is an arrangement of fixed pieces, it is decorative, and I did not think of myself as either fixed or part of a decoration. This Canadian mosaic, if that's what it was, consisted of leaky pieces streaking colours and patterns into each other, changing constantly while headed towards... something different and new. To go further, the pieces of this leaky mosaic were themselves shifting. Immigrants do not cross thousands of miles proposing to remain the same, whatever their own wishes (and they are often contradictory) or their public portrayals are. But they need time to evolve, each group in its own way. Some, like Neil Bissoondath, author of the bestselling book *Selling Illusions*, a critique of official multiculturalism, make a strong case for cutting all ties with the past and starting afresh as one hundred percent Canadians; others come with strong communal and religious ties and historical memories, not to say their own languages and cuisines, and they take time to grow and resolve their contradictions and contribute to the overall change in society. Already within a few years, in some of the communities that arrived in Trudeau's 1970s, mixed marriages were on the rise; heritage languages—former mother tongues—were being forgotten or getting adjusted, despite government efforts to help preserve them, as were the imported English accents often incomprehensible to natives; foods were undergoing transformation and compromise. Gays and lesbians were more readily accepted, when traditionally they were frowned upon, ridiculed, and ostracized.

Was there, then, a new breed of Canadian emerging? Perhaps—someone with a larger awareness of the world and an acceptance of different cultures. Some people were more accepting of change and difference than others, but in the larger cities the faces on the street, the languages spoken, the music heard, and the foods available were now of great variety. A single nation, with many cultures, many peoples coexisting. This is the new Canadian reality. But being aware and accepting of other cultures and races does not imply living close to them physically or mentally; it does not imply sharing opportunities readily; it does not get rid of racism and all the inherited phobias against the others. It does not get rid of habits of exclusiveness and received memories of dominance and privilege.

The "Canadian" and Other Creatures

Most of us possess a series of identities that tell us who we are in addition to being citizens of our country. These other identities—religious, racial, national origin, ethnic—impart to us our sense of self. Immigrants become proud Canadians once they land, but what are they in their hearts and minds? The qualifier is often all too important.

For a long time after I came to Canada, whenever I heard immigrants speak among themselves of "the Canadians," they meant "white." Over the years this habit of speech has loosened somewhat, but the distinction between "us" and "them" persists and slips out even decades after arrival. We might expect that ethnic or racial identities would have become less significant with greater familiarity among peoples, and yet they have remained, enforced by persistent racism: virulent or mild, it has sought out difference and division. They are aided by, I would add, that ubiquitous mode of instant communication, the internet. And the category "Historically Disadvantaged" on official forms, though well-meant, further retains that division, at least for the present.

By "Canadian" is often meant not only white but those specifically of Anglo-Saxon or French heritage, who have long dominated public power and prestige and claimed for themselves the title of "Founding Nations." (Presumably the rest of us are the confounding nations.) In English Canada, Anglo-Saxon or WASP is an ethnicity implicit and unspoken, and yet assertive, and it has its manners and its culture and bears the benefits of the historical privilege of the former ruling class. Everyone else is ethnic but the WASP.[4] A similar situation prevailed for long in the United States, which is why Hollywood actors used to adopt Anglo-Saxon-sounding names. The glamorous Rita Hayworth (Margarita Carmen Cansino) and the charismatic Kirk Douglas (Issur Danielovitch Demsky) come to mind here. (In India, Muslim actors used to adopt upper-caste Hindu names in order to be accepted widely.) Ironically, in Canada and the US the differences and divisions once imposed by the dominant WASP group are now retained emphatically by the once-dominated to seek recognition and redress. A name like Ta-Nehisi Coates or Amiri Baraka would have been unthinkable in the public domain in the past.

Religious faith may loosen with time in the face of easier lifestyles and broader access to knowledge that rationalizes our world and our experiences; for many Canadians of European descent religion is now only a very secondary feature of their lives. In the larger cities, at least, one doesn't think of a white Canadian as a Christian first; one does not question their denomination—they may not be a Christian at all but Buddhist or atheist or a recent convert to Islam or Sikhism. And yet for those Canadians of more recent vintage, faith gets strengthened by displacement, as people cling more closely to the God they brought with them. There is an entrenchment of religious identity and devotion. Global politics, local racism, the insecurity of displacement, the hustle and loneliness of modern life, the breakup and dispersal of extended families: all these are factors that push people to seek community through their ancestral faiths and cultural practices. Mosques and temples flourish, as do "ethnic" churches. Moreover the internet has enabled communities to discover, invent, or embellish their histories and propagate them across the globe in order to assert and strengthen their identities, which had lain obscured for decades or even centuries.[5] There is strength in numbers and the reach is global—and yet it is often narrowly sectarian or communal. What gives us the world also pulls us into a box. Do we then have a nation of compartments? This is what some have feared.

Multiculturalism and Its Discontents

The term "multiculturalism" was touted when I arrived as a uniquely Canadian invention. But as many immigrants could have told the "Canadians," the idea was hardly new; it existed in implicit practice in many parts of the world. In Dar es Salaam, where I grew up, you could daily hear bells from Hindu temples and the adhan from various mosques, or witness on special days a Swahili wedding procession going down a street with trumpet blaring, or the Ismaili scout band marching to Sousa. We grew up speaking Kutchi and Gujarati at home, English in school, and Swahili was the lingua franca. India, where our ancestors came from, is itself a nation of many cultures and languages and has numerous religious public holidays. But the term "multiculturalism" had cachet in Canada. The government's multiculturalism directorate oversaw grants for projects of "multicultural" value: a picture book of family or community history was in, but abstract poetry by an immigrant was out; dance, music, and food fairs naturally were also in, if they were sufficiently "ethnic."

A trenchant critique of multiculturalism—in the Canadian context—was published by Neil Bissoondath in his aforementioned book, *Selling Illusions: The Cult of Multiculturalism in Canada*, which came out in 1994, and in a second edition in 2002. A writer of fiction and an essayist of Indian ancestry born in Trinidad, Bissoondath had just broken onto the Canadian literary scene with much fanfare. *Selling Illusions* is well-meant and passionately argued on behalf of Canada, and expresses the author's disappointment at the direction in which the country seemed to be heading with the concept of multiculturalism as its compass. It was a national bestseller, lauded by those who saw multiculturalism taking Canada's culture to the dogs, and reviled by liberal activists who saw multiculturalism as a validation of minority cultures and rights. It may seem dated now, overtaken by the more recent tumultuous events and the resulting changes in cultural and political attitudes; nevertheless there is enough in it of relevance to think about.

For Bissoondath, the Multiculturalism Act of 1971 was purely a political expediency, passed when Prime Minister Pierre Trudeau and the Liberals were losing popularity in the country, its purpose being to garner "ethnic" votes and to dilute Quebec's claim to special status in the Canadian confederation. The Act recognizes the ethnic diversity of Canada and undertakes specifically to take measures to "encourage and assist individuals, organizations and institutions to project the multicultural reality of Canada . . . and encourage the preservation, enhancing, sharing and evolving expression of the multicultural heritage of Canada . . . [and] provide support to individuals, groups or organizations for the purpose of preserving, enhancing, and promoting multiculturalism in Canada."[6]

Bissoondath objects to the government's activism, as expressed by this Act, which he calls naive, disarming, and sentimental. Much ink is spent by the author in highlighting the excesses and ludicrousness that the easygoing, government-aided multiculturalism sometimes led to. No doubt these were there. An easy one to ridicule was the Caravan festival in Toronto, a food fair where people strolled about tasting different "ethnic" cuisines while being exposed to amateur shows and exhibitions. There was a quaintness to this sunny event, but it provided an outing for ordinary people, many of whom were new to the country and did not know or could not afford other forms of entertainment. It was also a way for cultures that had been far apart globally at least to introduce each other. Bissoondath imagines that thereby, with government encouragement, cultures became commodified and stale while remaining forever in their separate boxes. This could only be the view of someone who lived divorced from any cultural community and could not see its inevitable evolution over the years.[7] Such colourful ethnic-centred entertainments as Caravan were but minor engagements in the lives of immigrant communities struggling to survive and adapt while preserving what they could of what they had brought.

Multiculturalism when I arrived in Canada from the United States implied to me a mood of tolerance for difference and a warning against racist discrimination. This was enough. I had neither read the Act nor knew its language until recently, in Bissoondath's book. None of the people I came across in the arts scene knew it as much else. More importantly, to the large immigrant communities of Don Mills, Scarborough, and Mississauga in Greater Toronto and those in Calgary and Vancouver, among whom were members of my extended family, it hardly meant anything. All they wanted from this abstraction called multiculturalism was to be left alone to adapt to their new country in their own ways. For their cultural programs and festivals they collected donations from their members, and their events were attended by the hundreds. The Vishnu temple, the Ithna-Asheri community centre, the Ismaili Centre and Aga Khan Museum, the Muslim mosque in Thorncliffe Park, all in Toronto, and similar centres across the country were not built with government money in aid of "multiculturalism."

Bissoondath does not fail to condemn Canada's history of racism, and the xenophobia of colonial holdouts who hark back to the bygone exclusionary era of an Anglo-French Canada. What he fears is the racial and communal divisiveness of the kind he had casually witnessed in the Trinidad of his youth, and he condemns what he sees as the government's promotion and entrenchment of it through its much-vaunted Multiculturalism Act. He does not want another label besides "Canadian." Forget roots, forget history. Submerge your culture.

Was this ever possible anywhere?

"My roots," he says, "travel with me, in my pocket as it were, there to guide or succour me as need be." But roots are not like some dead tubers in the pocket. And history is not portable and of the moment, like a schedule or a map to consult at will. History is lived in people's lives and ties them into communities. It is ancient history and recent memory and an essential part of their identity.

As examples of divisiveness he looks with disdain at the "sticking with your own kind" phenomenon that he sees at the York University cafeteria, students of Chinese and South Asian backgrounds gathering in large numbers of separate groups at the tables, apparently oblivious of the others; he does not wonder why they would behave in this manner. At the same time he quotes with approval Christian Dufour's explanation of why Quebecers still hold to their hearts their defeat by the English at the Plains of Abraham (at the site of Quebec City) two hundred years ago: "Contrary to the vanquished, the conquered is affected to the heart of his collective identity." Surely the same can be said of any colonized or oppressed people—the Black descendants of slaves, the Jewish survivors of the Holocaust, the Indigenous Americans, victims of the Indian Partition and Apartheid South Africa. We come bearing complexes and insecurities. Histories.

The students Bissoondath mocks as they sit and stand rowdily at cafeteria tables, speaking in their mother tongues, also carry memories of colonial history, of defeat and conquest and racism in their homelands. They have faced racism in their neighbourhoods in Canada. Their parents have set up homes and go forth on the bus and subway every morning to work or seek jobs in a racist-tinged atmosphere. Such was the racism in Toronto in the 1970s and 80s (two violent incidents to my knowledge besides the jeering and casual discrimination) that when, while at Chalk River, I was offered a chance to come for a job in Toronto, I seriously debated with myself if I should accept. ("Paul, should I go?" I asked my senior colleague Paul Lee at Chalk River Nuclear Labs. "What?" he replied, somewhat too loudly for comfort, "afraid of Paki-bashing?" Obviously no help.)

"For a long time now, I have thought of Trinidad as simply the place where I was born . . . After half a lifetime away from the island, I have no emotional attachment left . . ."

Few people would say that about where they grew up, even when they had to depart as exiles, with bitterness or grief, leaving all behind, sometimes centuries of history. These places often hold their dearest memories. Literature is full of stories about growing up from a state of innocence—Marcel Proust,

V. S. Naipaul, Maxim Gorky, Wole Soyinka, Sherwood Anderson, Mahatma Gandhi, and so on. A writer of fiction need not be reminded that the past lives in him. In Canada, we have seen evocations of childhood in the Caribbean in the fiction of Cyril Dabydeen, Arnold Itwaru, Harold Sonny Ladoo, Shani Mootoo, and Ramabai Espinet; the stories are bleak, emerging from the Indo-Caribbean experience of indentureship, but they are literature and important as histories. (This may reflect my own ignorance, but I've not come across depictions of happy childhoods in this genre. A sad legacy of colonialism.)

The year 1988 was the 150th anniversary of the first arrival of indentured Indians in the Caribbean and it was commemorated in Toronto and other places with cultural programs and conferences. The celebration was not of the hardships but of coming together and remembering and recording. *The Toronto Review* came out with a 256-page dedication issue, with fiction, poetry, and essays. The essays revealed historical information new to most people; the fiction evoked the lives of indentured Indian labourers; the poetry showed the literary skills of their descendants. One could rightly argue that only in a few places, one of them being Canada, would such an event and dedication be possible.

Community cultural events, in general, may not be as serious in intent; but they provide important release and succour to stressed, displaced, suburban populations. The children's dances are crudely amateurish, the Bharat Natyam seems stilted, the imitations of Bollywood somewhat pathetic, the dandia folk dance not as brisk and colourful as the practised versions of Gujarat. (Imitating Michael Jackson's moonwalk was a favourite boys' act when I arrived.) But surely there will always emerge a few young folk who will train professionally, potential here for new creations to burst forth. A few years ago the talented professional dancer Hari Krishnan, for example, was commissioned to choreograph a classical Indian dance routine as a memorial to the beloved Canadian Tamil academic Chelva Kanaganayakam of Trinity College, Toronto, who had suddenly and tragically passed away. It was a brilliant dance and a resounding success (performed at the Miles Nadal Jewish Community Centre). One might well call it a truly Canadian dance.

The immigrants came to Canadian cities, choosing to live in close proximity to people like them, so they could turn to each other in their loneliness and bewilderment as they adjusted their lives and expectations. From such "ghettos" and community groups emerged in a couple of decades a Lieutenant Governor of a province, a major-city mayor, many doctors (including epidemiological specialists during the Covid crisis), members of Parliament, university professors, CEOs, and major donors to public charities. It is this long view that Bissoondath refused to see in his fear and criticism of multiculturalism's divisiveness.

However, one may take issue with some of his observations, but were his fears and warnings of a divided nation true? That depends from which side of the lens one looks. More of that later.

M.G. VASSANJI

Multiculturalism and Quebec

Multiculturalism was a philosophy that Quebec seemed to reject. Bissoondath shows much understanding for the province's position, as his quote above from Christian Dufour illustrates, but he is also quick to point out its xenophobia and excesses. But Quebec is distinct, he asserts, in its history, its culture, its language. No Canadian would deny that. He became conscious of it at a university course on Québécois literature, which he found "striking in its intensity," and later chose to move to Quebec City where he found that he was readily accepted; with his wife he brought up a daughter there. According to him, the Multiculturalism Act was a political move to diminish Quebec's status and he casts doubt on the importance Pierre Trudeau actually gave to it. (Apparently, in his memoir, Trudeau didn't mention it once.) Bissoondath quotes the writer and publisher Lise Bissonnette: "Carried over into Quebec, this multiculturalism would be suicidal, since it tends to make francophones a minority like the others." This is surely overblown, referring to a province with a population, in the year the book was published, of 7.4 million (Canada's was 31.4 million). And who exactly are the "others"? Moreover, "minority" is how you define it: to the non-white Canadians, white Québécois would be a genuine part of the white majority.

There was a time—say the 1970s and 80s—when most immigrants would have seen Quebec as Canada's particular strength, giving a special flavour to an essentially humdrum (but safe) country where the Queen of England was quaintly the head of state. Bissoondath quotes the writer J. B. Priestley saying, "A Canadian is lost when he is asked what a Canadian is."[8] Many immigrants who arrived in the 1970s enrolled their children in French-immersion school programs, and I recall instructing my two sons how important French was. The rejection of Quebec separation in the referendum of 1995 was greeted with joy and relief by everyone I knew. But it is only in Quebec now that I feel somewhat foreign; where with a Bank of Montreal credit card and two loud sons in tow, obviously speaking English, I was asked at a restaurant when paying the bill, "Where do you come from? India?" The server was a young woman, perhaps from a small town—what would she know about the rest of Canada? We smiled and explained. Another time it was at the little museum in Tadoussac. (We had, in fact, recently published in translation a young Innu poet from that region.) The questioner here was an elderly woman, and this was a small town (with a long history); we had no doubt she meant where in the world we came from—but why should we feel aggrieved? I've never taken umbrage at such questions (as others have done); to me they are not micro or nano aggressions, and I am only too happy to inform the curious that I live in Toronto, came from Africa, having stayed eight years in the US before, three of my grandparents and my great-grandfather came from western India in Gujarat, from the towns of Jamnagar, Una, and Porbandar and . . . I could go on. Nevertheless, where we once thought Quebec added a special, unique, and essential flavour to Canada, without which the country would be as plain as a chapati, now with a few million newcomers having arrived in the last few decades, with cities such as Toronto and Vancouver spiced with new colour, sounds, and cuisines, the Quebec flavour exudes a fainter whiff. Many might view it as the complaining province, a part of the body politic always in pain. At a small literary festival in Berlin celebrating Canadian literature to which I was invited, a Quebec author, apparently well known, attacked me as soon as we met, with verbiage including the word multicultural. I had done nothing to provoke her, but somehow she found my presence there, representing literary Canada, problematic. It could have been my face (I have a beard), but I was not bothered, I knew who I was and where I came from—Toronto, Dar es Salaam, Gujarat, etc. I have forgotten that author's name.

Does the Centre Not Hold?

Was Bissoondath's warning correct—that "the centre of the nation's being" was being "effaced" by the "transitions created, to a large degree, by multiculturalism"? In other (my) words, Canadian identity was becoming fractured. He says later, more affirmatively, "The historic centre and the sense of national self it offered are, for all intents and purposes, no more. A void remains." What was the alternative, use police to enforce "assimilation"—whatever that is?

Over twenty years after the book's publication, a column in the *Globe and Mail* of December 14, 2018 resoundingly declared on the basis of a poll that the evidence is that Mr. Bissoondath was wrong. Attachment to ethnic groups is declining precipitously, national identity has remained strong, immigrants quickly adapt to Canadian values, opposition to immigration is half what it was in the early 1990s, and Canada now has the highest percentage of foreign-born inhabitants since 1921 ... The country shows every sign of having solved the postmodern riddle of diversity that has torn Europe and the US apart.[9]

This conclusion, though partly true—of course there is greater visible diversity in the city streets—is also overblown, giving us a statistician's bird's-eye view of reality, missing the cracks and corners. Laying aside what is meant by "Canadian values," a term insulting and patronizing to new Canadians (do they emerge from lawless places devoid of human values? What is so special about Canadians' values that other humans don't share?) and already "othering" them, the conclusion also demonstrates the wishful thinking typical of white liberal Canada to show how much better we are than other countries, especially the United States. The answers of a new immigrant would naturally be defensive, made to please the ears of the white young liberal "Canadian" asking a loaded question in a poll. Canada's mainstream culture, as I have already pointed out, was until recently overwhelmingly white and Anglo- or French-European; it is remarkable that European Canadians were so blind to this feature for so long. The other cultures were suburban, played their roles in a minor key to the theme of Canada the great, modern, good, liberal nation. Anti-Muslim sentiments had been whipped up by the Harper national government[10] (which departed in 2015), and while intermarriages were also on the rise—though I would argue that they were selective—communal and religious identities had at the same time strengthened.

The article moreover ignored (as did Bissoondath) the Indigenous issue, which was waiting round the corner to blow up; just as it ignored the historical grievances of the Black communities, which had been heightened recently by more police murders of Black people down south and would soon lead to eruptions of protests from the Black Lives Matter and other movements. And as I have pointed out, small communities were reaching out across the globe, over the internet, to people of similar backgrounds to strengthen their other identities.

In the years 2020–21, with the growing awareness of the abuses of the residential school system (3200 children are reported to have died) and its presumptive ideology ("To eliminate any separate Indigenous identity"[11]), and as more bodies of Indigenous children were discovered, Canadians, aghast at these revelations, were now faced with the dark history of the land. (Though the revelations, in their substance, were hardly new.) The question of who and what was a Canadian now loomed as never before. The Indigenous nations had long protested against the celebration of Canada Day (July 1, the date in 1867 when the country was declared a Confederation); in the light of the Indigenous issue, many people now began to question the validity of this commemoration: what were we actually celebrating? By 2022 the celebrations had begun to alter "in the spirit of reconciliation"—Winnipeg and Halifax were even renaming it "A New Day"[12] (whatever that signifies). And most of us were now told we were merely settlers on a colonized land, just like—and one may not like to hear this—the white settlers of Rhodesia (Zimbabwe), Kenya, South Africa, and other colonies.

We have become, willingly or not, more conscious than ever before of who we are besides Canadians. Official forms, often with enticements to redress historical abuse and neglect, give us a list of identities to pick from: Asian, Black, Indigenous, LGBTQ, etc., and sometimes even smaller categories. Jobs, prizes, bank loans may depend on one's label. Naturally the white majority would largely resent this outcome; and naturally too some would wonder how "coloured" need they be to qualify for a benefit. Are Somalis and Ethiopians Black enough? Are Syrians and Albanians white?

There is no doubt then that in recent times Canada has become more fragmented. Could it be otherwise? What kind of identity or "sense of self" did it have in the past except as a distant dominion of the empire and a subservient neighbour to a growing, belligerent superpower? What we have now, instead, is a clamour of voices, all seeking redress and recognition. One cannot wish away the stinging memories of racial domination and colonization, or ignore the vast global inequalities in wealth and populations that drive people osmotically, naturally to wealthier shores. The question remains, can we evolve from all this a new sense of national self and identity, despite our differences, that embraces all our histories? Recently a good friend of mine who is Black and an astute literary critic told me, referring to our different backgrounds, "You can never know what you don't know." This was deeply wounding, for it told me we could never get closer. Our histories separated us.

4

Patriotism and Loyalty

To possess multiple group identities is now a commonplace concept; these identities may include race or ethnicity, religion, caste, sex and sexual orientation, political or ethical beliefs, all usually subsumed under one's national identity. A Canadian can be many other things.[1] This is the premise behind the nation's vaunted diversity and the plurality of its society. Canada's constitution guarantees equal rights to all its citizens; its policy of multiculturalism—whether as the federal Act or a government advisory—encourages the retention of the nation's many cultures and by implication promotes equal public space and representation to all its ethnicities and cultures. Whether this is entirely possible, given historic biases, is another matter. Institutional bias may be rectified, but inherited personal prejudice tends to linger.

Conflicts often arise—small or large, soluble or insoluble—resulting from one's identities. The details of who you are then matter. During the First World War, having German or Austrian origins became a liability in Canada; similarly, having Japanese origins during the Second World War. In the aftermath of the 9/11 attacks on Manhattan and Washington DC, Muslims in the United States (and to a lesser degree in Canada) were subjected to harassment, detention, and even physical attacks. (The term "Islamophobia" has since been invented.) In Pakistan, ever since the nation declared itself, in its new constitution of 1973, as an Islamic republic, its small Ahmadiyya sect has lived an even more precarious existence as "non-Islamic." (It was simply a minority Muslim sect before.) Colonial occupation in previous centuries left more conflicts in its wake, having imposed artificial boundaries in Asia and Africa, so that upon liberation, people of the same ethnic group found themselves in different countries. Thus the Masai in modern Kenya and Tanzania. In Punjab and Bengal, a single people (in the ethnic sense) were identified as Muslims and Hindus, which division gave cause to the Partition of India in 1947 and the creation of Pakistan, followed by perpetual hostility and three wars. Elsewhere the world saw the forced "population exchange" between Greece and Turkey (1923), the expulsion of Germans from Eastern Europe following World War II, the Ugandan Asian expulsion of the early 1970s.

To those of us in modern times who find ourselves split by and spread across land and sea boundaries for any number of reasons, a morally attractive position might be that of cosmopolitanism, or world-citizenship, in which one identifies first and foremost with the community of human beings everywhere, overriding one's commitments to one's current or former country of residence and citizenship or anything else. The ethics scholar Martha Nussbaum is a strong proponent of this idea, which is debated by a number of authors in her provocative collection titled *For Love of Country: Debating the Limits of Patriotism*. In her own essay advocating cosmopolitanism, she quotes several great thinkers of the past, including the Roman philosopher Seneca, who wrote, "we look neither to this corner nor to that, but measure the boundaries of our nation by the sun."[2]

Of course Seneca could be speaking as an imperialist, over whose domain (with a nod to Winston Churchill) the sun was presumably never expected to set. But the idea and the sentiment are ancient, as Nussbaum argues. She writes, explicating her position, "To count people as moral equals"—as she does, as a cosmopolitan—"is to treat nationality, ethnicity, religion, class, race and gender as 'morally irrelevant...'"[3] Great literature, she goes on, from Shakespeare to Dante to Tagore, because its appeal is across nations, is cosmopolitan. (There are, however, strong arguments against universalism in literature, as I've pointed out in a later chapter.) But her position is both laudable and contentious, and most of her contributors take exception to it, making cases in favour of patriotism as being more or equally important for the integrity of a nation.

Patriotism has been defined as taking on the responsibilities of citizenship, or taking on full-heartedly the ideals of the nation, or committing oneself with others in the mutual enterprise of nationhood. "We cannot do without patriotism," says Charles Taylor, the only Canadian in the debate, for to participate in democratic projects requires "a special sense of bonding."[4] This is a studied notion, a rational, commonsensical prescription for good citizenship that one can hardly argue with. The American philosopher Richard Rorty elsewhere puts this idea slightly differently, saying, "National pride is to countries what self-respect is to individuals, a necessary condition for self-improvement."[5] However, these philosophical ideas expounded from a high perch do not explain the emotions so frequently associated with the term and made evident daily in the lives of people. Patriotism is more commonly felt as a sentiment; it is love, as the poet Robert Pinsky says, for one's "homeland or group," and the "pull of the parental home."[6] How many writers have waxed lyrical over their homeland; one thinks of Wordsworth and Walt Whitman, and Muhammad Iqbal's "Of all the world, my Hindustan is best," sung daily by schoolchildren in India.

The fervor of patriotism is starkly observed at public events and on national days. In the United States we see it in something as innocuous as a sports final, where the national colours are on full display, the military is prominently present, and the anthem sung in a performance, joined by spectators full of emotion, their hand to their breast. To the rest of us, it is either an enviable or a frightening sight. During the World Cup soccer tournament, which is held every four years, fans travel long distances to watch their countries perform, emotions are at fever pitch, tears flow, of joy and sorrow. The national anthems are sung with gusto, the national colours are on display, but thankfully the military is absent. The Olympic Games are opened with national parades, medals are tallied back home, anxieties are raised, new heroes are made. In the spring of 2018, Toronto erupted with joy when its basketball team, the Raptors, won the

NBA championship. Thousands of ecstatic young people gathered outside the stadium and cheered with abandon. T-shirts appeared celebrating the team and individual players became household names. Were one to ask such a lover what it was about his team that he adored, he would be as stumped as a man who is asked what he loved about his beloved. It is one thing or another, even the flaws.

It is patriotic sentiment that makes a young man or woman volunteer to lay down their life for their country. But such patriotism can easily curdle into phobia of the other, be they of Canada or not. To kill an enemy soldier, plunge a bayonet into his gut or spray him with bullets or fire a rocket at him, one has to dehumanize him first. During my months of National Service in Tanzania, one of the motivating rhythmic chants we sang during our morning jog was "Kill!"—kill the enemies of Africa, taken by name, one by one. (This was a time when wars of liberation were underway in South Africa, Mozambique, and Angola.) We've seen dehumanizing practices in our media and we've seen it in the movies. The enemy was German—the "Hun" or the "Bosch"— and the Japanese—the "Jap" or the "Gook"; later it was the Russian, and later still the Muslim. Even now, I cannot remove that hint of a shadow left behind by Hollywood in my younger days when I imagine a German (*The Great Escape*, *Hogan's Heroes*) or a Japanese (*The Bridge on the River Kwai*).

But what if one's passion is for two lovers simultaneously? The 1945 film *Brief Encounter* movingly portrays the dilemma of a young married woman who meets a man at a train station and falls uncontrollably in love. Nevertheless she is also devoted to her husband, who gives her stability and a home—and a love of sorts. Fortunately for the two lovers (and the film's denouement), the man (Trevor Howard) gets a job in Kenya and the woman (Celia Johnson) goes back to her normal life with her memories.

The immigrant in a new country often is caught between two lovers; in this case, too, some deception may be called for. The Nigerian Canadian poet James Yékú puts this conflict succinctly: "You may leave Nigeria, but it never truly leaves you. Nigeria feels like a perpetual space in your soul . . ."[7] Substitute India for Nigeria, and many Indians will echo the same mantra.

In 1990 the British Conservative politician Norman Tebbit, troubled that members of non-white communities cheered the Caribbean and Indian and Pakistani cricket teams in their matches against the home (England) team, coined the term and concept "cricket test" as a measure of loyalty.[8] Many fans were failing that test, evidently, and once the politician's remarks had been published, the accused somewhat gleefully and defiantly continued to cheer their teams of choice. Clearly the young people, born in England, were English and simply exercising the freedoms their country's laws gave them. Reasons for their displays could be various: reactions to racism in the county cricket clubs or in the country as a whole (the England cricket team until recently has always been almost all white), or pull from their ancestral identity, which is still a part of who they are. (I would venture that in Canada and the United States such shows of "disloyalty" would not be tolerated by the public.

Immigrants would pretend, if need be, to cheer the local side unequivocally.)

The immigrant's centre is different—or rather, he has been decentred—consequently, his world is different and larger than that of the native Canadian. Intellectually he finds himself in a bind. Objectivity about the world comes naturally to one who's chosen to leave his birthplace for personal reasons. It feels more honest to be able to say, All countries have good and bad moments, no country is the best; or, Today I support the other team because it is the underdog. Politically and morally there are other sides to an issue, perspectives unavailable to a native steeped in Western histories and unquestioned prejudices. What better example of this frustrated, conflicted observer than the Somali taxi driver I once met, evidently educated (perhaps a doctor or engineer in a former life), whose taxi job had provided him with a keen metaphor for his life; in his new profession, with time to kill on the road at night he accessed news and analyses from multiple sources around the globe in several languages on his radio. An almost-cosmopolitan.

Such an immigrant, and there are many like him, educated and arrived from what used to be called the third world—which was an identity with an ideology of non-alignment, fighting poverty, imperialism, and apartheid—might be called a "cosmopolitan" in a limited sense, identifying not with the entire human race, as Martha Nussbaum would advocate, but certain regions of the world. When I meet in Toronto or Vancouver or Calgary a man from Somalia (who may know some Swahili) or Ghana or the former Yugoslavia who has heard of Julius Nyerere of

Tanzania, a certain recognition falls into place, a bond is admitted. We might discuss the World Cup, Barack Obama, the political situation in parts of Africa, the rule of Kwame Nkrumah in Ghana, Marshal Tito, or why Tanzania is admired as one of the most stable countries in Africa.

Assimilation is blithely offered to immigrants as the path to settling and integrating in their new country. All that means is that certain basic civic values and laws be respected. It does not mean an erasure of memory. (Though this was often what was required in the past from Indigenous Peoples.) One cannot assimilate one's skin colour or instantly adopt a new accent (though some try). It takes some adaptation to realize that Canada has its English spoken in a variety of accents. (Recently my son, born and bred in Toronto, spoke of a person at his workplace who had an Eastern [Maritime Canadian] accent.) One evening, sitting on my porch, venting my silent frustration at this idea offered so blithely—"Assimilate!" "Integrate!"—I mused to myself, Wouldn't it be convenient if one could erase one's memory? All one's conflicts of loyalty and difference, all those painfully dear boyhood memories would be gone. There would be no need to pretend that I came from a terrible place in the "developing world" to this heaven called Canada, no need to defend that other place. Once I heard, to my outrage, a CBC television anchor casually compare Mombasa to the "black hole of Calcutta," an insult to both cities. Mombasa, where my mother grew up, is a historic city, a home to many races and cultures, where in 1498 the Portuguese sailor Vasco da Gama arrived and picked up two Indian men to guide him onward to the Malabar Coast in India; Calcutta is one of the most cultured cities on the earth. That night on the porch in that frustrated state I fantasized about a world in which one could erase old, unwanted memories and replace them with other, chosen ones in order to take on a more acceptable, painless identity in this new country and become a new person. Telltale physical features would be altered, there would be no sign left of that other man—the Indian African Canadian. That thought, years later, became my novel *Nostalgia*.

Conflicts may arise between values brought by the immigrants with those of the host nation, but there are ways to resolve them. (When Tanzanian Asians arrived in the 1970s to live in the apartments and condominiums in Toronto suburbs, the locals were outraged at men coming out in pajamas; the Asians on the other hand replied, What about your women coming out shamelessly on the lawn in knickers?) Sharia law, hijab, turbans, and kirpans—the Sikh ceremonial dagger—have given rise to controversies. But immigrants are not inherently immoral and violent. They love their new country, appreciate its bureaucratic efficiency, lesser blatant corruption, greater economic opportunities, access to health and education, and respect for basic human rights. Any visitor to Toronto's Thorncliffe Park will see people visiting the mosque in traditional garb or down the road see others proceed to another mosque in modern Western clothes. It should not be forgotten also that those who lay claim to "true" or authentic Canadian-ness are often harking back to ancestral links in Great Britain and France.

Memory is not easily erased. During the recent Covid pandemic, when a sense of mortality had so gripped much of the human race, when time seemed to have stopped, virtual features appeared—prayer services, health advice, culture programs, even cooking advice—keeping members of faith groups linked. Old, nostalgic photos circulated among chat groups—class groups, picnics, teachers, families—reviving the past, alongside news from "back there," which some had left four decades before. A few times I heard the question, Did we make the right move coming here? A fleeting thought at a desperate, depressing time when all about our lives was put to the test, and hardly to be taken literally—but surely also emerging from a real source within? The questions posed at that stressful time were existential: What in our lives is important, what do we run around for? Who are we, ultimately?

Years after the British politician Norman Tebbit proposed his cricket test of loyalty, he added that if it had been taken seriously, the terrorist bombings that took place in London in 2007 might have been prevented. The thought is absurd on several counts; for one, how would the test have been implemented? There is no reason to believe that those who "failed" his test did not consider themselves English.

The difference between "us" and "them" at a sports venue seems casual, but it can hide deeper divisions, the proverbial iceberg. There are those who see in their lives the debilitating residues of colonialism, imperialism, or slavery from the past, and the effects of continuing racism in the present. There are those who see their loyalties and passions in terms of race or religious faith or an ideology. These divisions could easily aggravate into full-fledged alienation from a common identity (we already see talk of "multipolarity") and a small minority seduced into thinking that violence, calculated or random, is the answer—either for change or revenge.

What I have in mind in particular, it should be obvious, is the disaffection of Muslims, especially the youth, in recent times. It is true that the London bombings and other acts of public violence in the early twenty-first century were conducted by those inspired by Al Qaeda's anti-West ideology.

Many Muslims worldwide believe that their co-religionists have been repressed across the globe by leaders of Muslim-majority countries who are aided by the West, and by the West itself, which colonized many of these countries in the recent past. That grievance is fuelled by racism at home and used by calculating fanatics to lure gullible, alienated young people into acts of violence in order to fight a so-called holy war in the name of Islam. Many such swayed young people have never even been to an Islamic country, some have only recently begun to identify with their ancestral faith, and some are new Muslims. But they all have the zeal of the fanatic.

But disaffection and alienation curdling into poison is not a new phenomenon; it has been around forever. We can begin with Guy Fawkes, who in 1605 with his cohorts almost succeeded in blowing up Parliament in London as a protest against the repression of Catholics. In our own times, the 1950s saw Americans Ethel and Julius Rosenberg charged with handing vital atomic weapons information to the Soviet Union (the charge was false and based on perjury in the case of Ethel, as has recently been revealed); their cause was communism.[9] Klaus Fuchs, a brilliant scientist who worked on the development of the nuclear bomb at Los Alamos, gave vital information to the Soviets that led to the development of their own weapon; his reason was mutual deterrence and the cause of world peace. The 1960s saw spies on both sides of the Iron Curtain engaged in acts of betrayal, the most famous of them the Cambridge Five in the UK. The 1970s and 80s saw European and Japanese terrorists running rampant with global causes. In the 1970s the Weathermen—young, white American men and women—carried out bombings for political causes. Indeed, it was not unusual to see American boys and girls, of the same ages as those who joined up with ISIS in the 2000s, carrying enemy North Vietnamese flags during anti-war demonstrations and chanting paeans to Ho Chi Minh. Even more recently, in January 2021, protesters, many of them carrying weapons, many of them veterans of the "War on Terror," attacked the United States Capitol. Now, ironically, though some of us had long predicted it, homegrown terrorism is considered by US authorities as a greater threat. Its ideology: white supremacy. Canadians need not feel smug. There was the FLQ movement of the 1960s for the liberation of Quebec that carried out bombings and kidnappings. And in later decades the many acts of mass violence against women and Muslims in Canada are surely also acts of terrorism.

In the 2000s the terror group ISIS attracted many bright young people, some of them as young as fifteen, into their fanatical cause. This was a tragedy, for the young people themselves, for their families, and for their countries. Instead of calling them names (an American politician on television called them cockroaches) one might well ask, what was it in our societies that caused this extreme disaffection in our brightest young minds?

Here I would like to consider how an assertive Islamic identity has been imposed on people, catching many of them quite unawares. (Geopolitical reasons are sometimes given[10] for this resurgence, but I am concerned with how it works at the ground level.)

Islam sees itself as a global religion; its mission is to all of humanity, its identity supposedly crosses borders. I grew up within a complex of small-sect Muslim (Ismaili), Indian (Gujarati), and national (Tanzanian and Kenyan) identities; the Indian Ismailism we practised was a syncretistic combination of mystical Hinduism and Islam, as I've explained in a later chapter. Over the years I turned agnostic and looked to my East African and Indian heritages to understand myself. Therefore I have always found it disconcerting how a Muslim woman in Kuala Lumpur or Abidjan, for example, would be—according to many people—more deserving of my concern (as a "sister") than my neighbour, born in Thessaloniki, Greece who keeps an eye on our house when we are away. (Of course, with the Malay woman I would always share the identity of a former colonized subject.)

Be that as it may, in recent decades several factors, I believe, have contributed to a growing assertion of the Muslim identity. Extremists, for one, claiming to speak and act for Islam and "Muslims," brought this label to the forefront of world discourse. Western media and governments responded to these shrill cries in the name of "Islam" and easily embraced the label as given to them in its general form. The extremists' form of Islam is, however, only one and practised—if one can call it that—by a few. But the threats were real and this apparently was no time for nuances. At the same time, fear of reprisals and resentment drove many people grudgingly under the Muslim umbrella: whether you're practising or not, even if you've left your former faith, you are afraid—of the security apparatus in your own country, of your neighbours, of the fanatics—and you're angry. Add to all that the shouts of Muslim activists, who resent any hint of disunity or nuance in the faith. Any demurral, any qualification is seen as denial, betrayal, self-hatred. All these factors have served to impose a Muslim identity on anyone who is even remotely, by the thinnest thread, connected with Islam. The public has been taught to see only "Muslims" and not people of different backgrounds—Arabs, South Asians, East Asians, Europeans, Iranians, Africans, Canadians, white Americans, Black Americans, etc.; devout, agnostic, or apostate; mystics or fundamentalists—connected in different ways to a certain creed. The label "Muslim" is then stuck on people to define them; and labels, as we know, are discriminatory, they highlight difference, bring forth stereotypes, misinformation, and ignorance, sometimes accompanied by fear and hatred.[11]

Why was the much-admired former mayor of Calgary referred to as a Muslim mayor (and why did he allow it), whereas the late Deepak Obhrai, also of Calgary, was never called a Hindu member of Parliament? Or Justin Trudeau a Christian prime minister? They are all Canadians first, and represent all Canadians. Philip Roth once asserted, regarding such labels, that he was an American writer who was a Jew, not a Jewish writer;[12] Mordecai Richler made a similar claim.

5

Writing to Somebody, Somewhere: The Telling Is Not Easy

The sense or awareness of an audience is intrinsic in what a writer produces, it has a role in how the content and the experience of a work—aesthetic, emotional, intellectual— are conveyed. It is often argued, nevertheless, that good literature autonomously is effective across cultures, it can have the same or similar impact whether you are a reader in Manitoba or a sheikh in Timbuctoo. We are human, goes the argument, wherever we come from, with the same sensibilities that can be touched. We all experience grief, joy, love, anger, envy, ennui. Therefore a work of art must be subject to the same criteria of appreciation whatever the background of its creator.

This is true to a degree, but at the same time just too easy. The purveyor of universality[1] usually sits in a position of protected privilege as a recognized cultural or academic commentator in a Western metropolis, learned in a single tradition (European) but ignorant of the complexities of that world out there—the inner and outer worlds of the immigrant, the exile, the many, many others who live across the seas in vastly diverse towns and villages. But a work becomes universal, as far as it can, only once it is understood. We are not entirely universal in our absorption of art and expressions of culture—even if we come from places such as Great Britain and America that have been able to spread their influences abroad. The subtleties of a modern English novel set in small-town Ontario, for example, would be difficult to grasp by an ordinary Tanzanian reader. That reader would struggle to understand the mores, the rituals, the psychology of a character whose roots lie in Protestant Christianity in England, Wales, or Scotland. The novelist Anthony Burgess, who taught for a period in Malaysia, wrote about his students' reception of the Western canon that

> both Dante and Shakespeare were less universal than I had previously believed. My students couldn't understand Dante's Catholicism and they had difficulty with the social customs of Shakespeare's England. I tried them on modern literature, and they laughed at Graham Greene. They couldn't see why the hero of *The Heart of the Matter* had to commit suicide because he couldn't stop committing adultery. "Why," said a bright Malay girl, "does he not become a Muslim like us and marry both women?"[2]

Every translator knows the impossibility of conveying a work with complete integrity into another language, another culture. Every generation in the West produces several new translations of its classics, ranging from Dante to Tolstoy, purportedly more relevant to the times. To read Rabindranath Tagore's *Gitanjali* in English translation, in my experience, is to wonder what it is in this poetry that makes Bengali readers and listeners swoon. (However, his collection *Stray Birds*, translated by himself, contains some strikingly beautiful lines.) Similarly, the beauty and power of the Urdu poems of Faiz Ahmed Faiz, another titan of twentieth-century South Asian literature, cannot be understood without explanations of their political contexts and classical imagery.

An immigrant writer comes from somewhere else. His audience exists, more and more, in his new environment. He brings with him memory, history, a philosophy of life—and much else that cannot be left behind like mere objects, such as clothes and pots and pans. This baggage of the mind is the raw material for his imagination. It is where he will start, or continue from, and no doubt his new experiences will inform his imagination and his work—as they would have done anywhere else. How does he convey the idiom and rhythm, the feel of a setting, the mode of thinking, the historical and cultural referents and urgencies that are unfamiliar to the culture and the medium he has chosen? How does he reach out and construct an audience? As the Indian novelist Raja Rao put it in a foreword to his great novel *Kanthapura*, written in English, "The telling has not been easy. One has to convey in a language that is not one's own the spirit that is one's own."[3] Rao wrote while resident in France; later he moved to Texas. In his novels, in his wonderfully sinuous prose he invokes and examines all the intricacies of mind and manners of traditional South Indian Brahmin life and what—according to him—it means to be an

Indian. If the telling, which is poetically beautiful, has not been easy, the reading is not easy either, for anyone.

Our writer cannot always use a shorthand or code with which to paint a scene, create a mood, imagine a character, set a historical, political, or cultural context in the manner a writer native to the culture and nation can. "Civil war" rings a bell full of implications for an American, an Englishman, or a Nigerian, but each hears a different sound. "Biafra" carries a resonance for Africans who are over a certain age. It certainly does for me, and I sometimes use it unconsciously to imply starvation, having seen, as a teenager, horrific pictures from the Nigerian civil war. (One of the few countries that recognized breakaway Biafra was Tanzania.) "Partition" evokes the cataclysmic tragedy of bloodshed and division, homelessness, murder, and rape to anyone from the Indian subcontinent. These references do not travel easily by themselves, without explanations. Most people in Canada would not know the extent of the tragedy that "Partition" signifies for north Indians, Bangladeshis, and Pakistanis. And so the writer has to elaborate and inform as he writes. He may create a city or village, a landscape, a community of people; he may describe their objects, introduce their history, articulate their thoughts, and present their ways of speech. To use a cliché, he tries to connect—to reach out to the reader, move him emotionally and intellectually, to make him see and empathize with another reality. He cannot lecture or make lists—an easy mistake. In the process, he discovers a suitable narrative form, finds a voice and rhythm, an idiom in English to echo as far as possible the idiom in which his creation comes to him; he adds meanings to the dictionary, pins places to the atlas. He makes the exotic sound mundane and familiar. And he defends his aesthetic.

The untutored (but confident) critic or reviewer might despair at this: he applies that beloved, though recent criterion of "spare prose" to a piece of work, and finds a fault. The writer, he further complains, using the well-worn cliché of the first-year writing seminar, "tells" but does not "show." He might add that there are too many characters, with no central protagonist. Theories of fiction are trotted out, as though creativity must follow established rules, like geometry. But, as we know from mathematics—to extend the analogy—there are many geometries besides Euclidean. To go from A to B one may enter a space of many dimensions before arriving. What appears as a curved line in one space is straight in another. Spare prose does not always work for a writer with baggage; Hemingway will not do here, however profound his evocation sounds. The stories the writer from elsewhere often tells are not merely about the individual, they are about the individual within a complex communal and linguistic structure, a matrix of relationships bound by traditions and existent within a history. Therefore the voices may be many, subtle strategies are devised to carry non-English vocabulary and insert different speech patterns and rhythms without offending the narrative. (This was done to some extent by Jewish writers, and to a larger, more exuberant extent by Salman Rushdie.) The writer may even pause to instruct. (Tolstoy of course did this in *War and Peace*.)

The Argentine writer Ernesto Sabato eloquently put it,

> A writer born in France finds, as it were, a homeland that already exists; in Latin America, he must write it at the same time he creates it, like the pioneers of the far west who farmed the land with a gun at their side.[4]

For "Latin American" we might simply substitute "immigrant" (and skip the gun).

I am reminded of the African writers who began producing poetry and fiction in English and French in the 1960s, soon after their countries' independence. Wole Soyinka, Chinua Achebe, Ngugi wa Thiong'o, Gabriel Okara, Okot p'Bitek, Cyprian Ekwensi, Taban Lo Liyong and numerous others, in an era of pulsating excitement on the continent, in defiance of the established literary traditions of Europe and America in which they had been tutored, brashly produced new, authentic works of literature in the colonial tongues, with their own idioms and sounds and ways of perception. Wole Soyinka's anthology, *Poems of Black Africa*,[5] is remarkable for its sense of newness and adventure, its generosity and diversity; even the concept of Blackness is extended. His own poem segment in the anthology powerfully evokes the sounds and images of his corner of Africa:

> Low beneath rockshields, home of the Iron One
> The sun had built a fire within
> Earth's heartstone. Flames in fever fits
> Ran in rock fissures, and hill surfaces

> Were all aglow with earth's transparency
> > Orisa-nla, Orunmila, Esu, Ifa were all assembled
> > Defeated in the quest to fraternize with man

It is a beautiful illustration of what Soyinka calls "the experience of the black Africa in the idiom of the poem," throwing out a challenge to every young African poet writing in English.

Often a writer's inspiration or calling comes from a need to recall. What is observed in childhood or youth informs his oeuvre in its spirit and its settings. Philip Roth drew on his childhood in the Weequahic section of Jewish Newark; Mordecai Richler set much of his work in the St. Laurent section of Montreal, known affectionately as "the Main," which he seemed never to have left even when he set a novel in the northwest of Canada. Ngugi wa Thiong'o in his novels used his childhood experiences of the Mau Mau insurgency in the Kikuyu region of Kenya; Naguib Mahfouz had Cairo; Soyinka had the Yoruba region of Nigeria.

For the immigrant or exile there arises a special poignancy in that he might not be able to visit that former home. Memory fades, reality on the ground changes, fake history emerges in the markets to create doubts in his mind. In his book *Austerlitz*, W. G. Sebald writes,

> . . . the darkness does not lift but becomes yet heavier as I think how little we can hold in mind, how everything is constantly lapsing into oblivion with every extinguished life, how the world is, as it were, draining itself, in that the

history of countless places and objects which themselves have no power of memory is never heard, never described or passed on.[6]

Sebald was concerned with another part of the world, with a consciousness that its story, at least over a certain period, had not been told. In his and in many other cases, history, consciously or otherwise, is then part of the literary project.

Looking back at East Africa, where I come from, there is much that could have been told and described about the past and filled the imagination of its people that is now lost forever. We have only fragments of myth and memory to tell us how people lived and died, grieved and celebrated, prayed and worshipped even a hundred years ago. We know little of the private lives and thoughts of those giants of African history, charismatic leaders like Kenyatta, Nyerere, and Nkrumah who were involved in the mid-twentieth-century struggles for national and continental independence. The few official and academic histories tell us of round-table conferences, provide dates, and record political speeches. (Recently, however, some memoirs and websites have appeared to remember forgotten history.)[7] The clamour and excitement of the "neo-colonial" years that followed is all but forgotten. Of the men and women involved all we have are anecdotes that change their shapes as easily as amoeba. Archives languish in disorder and are incomplete; entire eras go unrecorded. (Sixty years after independence, the once-imposing now decrepit McMillan Memorial Library in Nairobi, where archival material gathered dust in the basement when I last visited, is finally being restored.[8]) Wars disappear from memory. And the past gets reconstructed to suit the teller's needs. About pre-colonial days we read of the migrations of tribes, but not of the real, thinking and feeling people who moved from one region to another. We find numerous accounts of white explorers like Richard Burton, John Speke, David Livingstone, and H. M. Stanley who journeyed through Eastern Africa in the nineteenth century and became heroes and legends, but little is known about the men they met,[9] the suppliers, guides, and porters who were crucial to their survival. These explorers had abundant supplies of alcohol, they resorted to cruelty and violence, and during the months and years they spent travelling they slept with local women, though their published records are largely silent about this fact.[10]

It is left to the storyteller and poet to remember, to imagine and recreate, and thus to resurrect the past with some integrity and give history, memory and myth to his people.

6

Nowhere in Africa

Even as a child I did not know where exactly I belonged: Kenya or Tanzania? Was I a boy from the sophisticated, anglicized Nairobi of my family's memories or the backward Dar (Dar es Salaam) where we had come to live? I was born in the former, and grew up after the age of four and a half in the latter. My father's family was from Kenya, where they arrived in the late nineteenth century, my mother's from Tanzania, having arrived in Zanzibar only a little later. In Dar, where we had moved after my father's death, we never quite fitted in and always reminded ourselves that we were from Nairobi. Without a figurehead patriarch, we didn't quite have a presence and always felt like transients. My elder siblings had brought along their school blazers and ties, but they were of little use in the hot, humid weather of our new city; the habit of wearing shoes or sandals at home went away because we were poorer. Now early every morning we walked a couple of miles to school, and walked back in the afternoon heat, dusty, sweaty, and thirsty— pausing to beg at some shop a drink of water—whereas in the cool climate of Nairobi a school bus had taken us to and from. But when I went away to college in the United States, it was the streets of easygoing Dar that I missed the most, whose sounds still rang in my ear (they still do), though by then my family had moved back to Nairobi. When I first returned to Dar after nineteen years away, such was the emotion I carried that on my first morning there I trekked silently and purposefully, from seven till noon, unable to stop (except for a drink of Fanta) until I had reclaimed those streets I had thought were lost to me forever. Msimbazi Street, Uhuru Street (which also runs through my novels), Independence Avenue, Upanga Road, Boyschool (where the lab assistant Rajabu was still working), through United Nations Road and back to my host.

I grew up belonging to an exclusive Asian community, the Ismaili Khoja, one among several with ancestral memories of Gujarat, India, speaking two Indian languages in addition to the local lingua franca, Swahili. We also knew a smattering of Hindi, and English had just replaced Gujarati as the school medium of instruction, embraced readily as the prerequisite for advancement in life. Gujarat has a connection to East Africa going back to ancient times. Before the twentieth century, traders would arrive in dhows, brought by the trade winds across the Indian Ocean; the return passage was courtesy of the same winds when they reversed later in the year. Potters, I've been told, placed themselves with their earthenware on rafts and made the same return journey to Africa. In the late nineteenth and early twentieth centuries, following European colonization, larger numbers of Indians arrived to settle. The Germans, who colonized Tanganyika, and the British, who colonized Kenya and made Uganda and Zanzibar into "protectorates," found the

Asians useful in opening up the region to trade and administration. Starting out at Zanzibar or Mombasa, which were the ports of arrival, Asians spread out across East Africa such that the tiniest village would have at least one lonely Indian shop supplying daily essentials like oil and flour to the local Africans.

(Indians from Punjab were indentured in Kenya in the years 1896–1903 to build the railway from the Indian Ocean coast to Lake Victoria in Uganda.[1])

Dar es Salaam was a village when the bulk of Asian migration took place and is today a throbbing city of more than four million, gutted with car traffic. The area where they first settled, behind the harbour, which we called "gaam," became the downtown core, its maze of streets lined with two-storey buildings, the names of the owners' favourite sons or daughters carved or painted at the top. Under colonial rule, Europeans (whites), Asians (Indians), and Africans remained distinct, separate entities; the Africans had their exclusive tribes, the Asians their religious and caste communities. Each Asian community had its prayer house—temple, mosque, or jamat khana—and the cultural practices around it, brought over from India and evolving locally over the decades.[2]

What was home, then? It was no place else than this noisy world around us, the place where we had lived for two generations and more. But what *were* we?

We were Africans because our region of Africa was all we knew directly, it was the soil we grew up on, the landscape we knew intimately and can recall nostalgically. For me, growing up in Dar, my Africa stretched westward from the Indian Ocean to Lake Tanganyika (across which lay Congo); in the northwest lay the great Lake Victoria and to the southwest, Lake Nyasa. Kenya was to the north of us, and just inside the border rose the mighty snow-peaked Kilimanjaro, which I would stare at during the few times I travelled with my mother by bus to Nairobi, eyes glued to the window. There was also an abundance of wild animals to be seen. For a long time I carried visions of one day travelling—by road—from Nairobi to Lagos or Cairo to Cape Town. My Africa.

We were Africans, by any reasonable measure of belonging, but India too lived in us. I am tempted to say "lurked in us," because however much my generation—with eyes upon England as the epitome of civilization and the source of the best of everything—denied it as an embarrassment, India lived in us through our languages, our foods, our religious customs, and the many other tangibles and intangibles that define a people. Our mother tongues were Kutchi and Gujarati, though loaded with archaisms, as all spoken languages of migrants do, and inflected liberally with Swahili. Zanzibar, a boat ride away from Dar es Salaam, had gone a linguistic step or two further: it had evolved a distinctive Kutchi-Swahili patois: every other sentence spoken was a beautiful and perfect blend of the two. Swahili is a beautiful language, you love to speak it, it demands that you speak it, and it breaks all barriers—race, class, faith. We had adopted Swahili foods and included coconut-base corn, fish, cassava, and chicken dishes in our cuisine. (Correspondingly, chapatis, pilau, bhajia, and samosas had become integrated into the African cuisine of the coast.)

At the same time, legally, before independence we were British subjects and heavily influenced by British ways. At the cinema, a young Queen Elizabeth approaching on horseback was the first scene that came on the screen before the trailers and the main film; we would stand and the anthem would play. Even today, many of us can recite by heart "God Save the Queen" (and "Mungu ibariki Afrika" [God Bless Africa, the national anthem of Tanzania][3]). Cricket was a passion (Dar had more than ten cricket teams), tea was a staple, trifle pudding was an adapted delicacy for the wealthy, and "English" food (boiled or grilled) was considered healthy and enjoyed by the wealthy. The arrival of fish and chips to our town was an event of significance, a sign of progress à la Nairobi. Our schooling was in English and many of our schoolteachers were English. Our leisure reading came from Britain, and our final school exams were set and marked in Cambridge. Our daily newspaper brought us even more of that distant mother country: the death of Churchill, the Profumo affair, a grinning Chancellor of the Exchequer holding up his mysterious briefcase outside 11 Downing Street. The few who could afford to sent their kids to schools and colleges in England, to return as the haughty (so we thought) "London-returned."

And so we were a happy confusion of evolving, sheltered identities in a truly multicultural society, an Asian tribe in Africa influenced and tutored by Britain that was ultimately and inevitably hit by the rush of history that came with the force of a hurricane. Independence arrived for the African countries.

—

After independence, only a few Asians "returned" to India or Pakistan; fewer among them managed to stay there—they were too alien and stories spread of the horrors they saw. Many, especially from Kenya, went to the unwelcome embraces of England, where warnings of "rivers of blood" had gone up at the arrival of coloured former subjects of the empire. (Ironically, one of their descendants would become the future Chancellor of the Exchequer and prime minister of Britain.) It did not take the rest of us long to come to terms with reality and become patriots and champion the new, independent Africa. The yearning to belong somewhere could only be satisfied by acknowledging and embracing where we lived, who we were. Africa was exciting and its future looked bright. We—my generation—believed we were that future. Only one in ten children managed to get to high school, we were told; we, the privileged ones, were like the single child who is given all the food by a starving village to go away and bring back food for all. "Freedom from hunger!" and "Freedom with work! (Uhuru na kazi)" were the rallying cries. World leaders paid visits, so did Black activists from America. Freedom fighters of South Africa, Zimbabwe, Mozambique, and Angola operated from Tanzania.

The community I came from, the Khoja Ismailis (discussed in Chapter 8), had completely committed itself to Africa. Our leader, the imam, had exhorted us to lay our insecurities aside, "to go out of [our] way," to integrate, to become Africans. And that's all we were, two or more generations away from our ancestral homeland, which had since splintered. My parents had never seen India, and my mother happily—as advised by the community elders—returned her British-subject passport to the British High Commission.

We, especially the young people, were proud Africans and Tanzanians. During the holidays we volunteered to go and build homes outside the city, and travelled upcountry to count the national census; we joined the ruling party's Youth League and proudly wore its uniform—green shirt, black pants, and yellow scarf. I recall being taken to count votes at a Party convention, the President, Julius Nyerere, sitting not far away and acknowledging us. Nyerere was idolized; even today, walking along the streets of Dar, one might hear a taped, inspiring speech by him. He was an idealist, and incorruptible (but those under him weren't, which was the problem with the African Socialism that he brought us). With a master's degree from Edinburgh he had translated two Shakespeare plays into Swahili, one about his namesake, Julius Caesar. I have often wondered if, standing head and shoulders above fellow politicians, he was not inspired by the Roman consul into becoming a benevolent, beloved African dictator.

In school, during the heydays of the 1960s, we were encouraged to write stories and poems, to create a national literature; competitions were held, prizes given. African literature was burgeoning at that time, with names like Ngugi wa Thiong'o, Wole Soyinka, Chinua Achebe, Buchi Emecheta, Taban Lo Liyong, Gabriel Okara, and numerous others. The African Writers Series was launched by Heinemann from London and for more than two decades published many eminent writers from across the continent. Makerere University in Uganda became a major hub of this writing, and the world-renowned literary and cultural magazine *Transition* was founded there, edited by a Ugandan Asian called Rajat Neogi. V. S. Naipaul and Paul Theroux each spent a sabbatical year there, though not as part of the African writers' movement. Ngugi, called James Ngugi then, emerged from Makerere, and today is easily one of Africa's greatest living writers. Among his group at Makerere were three Asian Africans, two of whom were included by Wole Soyinka in his anthology *Poems of Black Africa*. One of them, Bahadur Tejani, also wrote a novel in which the protagonist agonizes over his Indian-ness, which he accepts with fervour, but still calls for a new Asian African identity.[4]

Still, Asians were a minority, easily identified, easily picked upon. Minorities make an easy target everywhere, too frightened to speak back or protest and therefore often not certain if they can ever truly belong. Picking on this nervousness, there was a tendency among unscrupulous politicians to bait the Asians, questioning their allegiance: were they Asian, African, or British? The majority of them running small shops, they were easily labelled "the Jews of Africa," raking in the money from the poor natives. The most insignificant politician could get away saying, "Go back to Bombay!" An MP in Kenya even warned Parliament in Nairobi that if this fast-breeding race went unchecked, the country would soon have an Asian president. Not only was this mathematically impossible, it went against the grain of the democratic ideals of his new nation. In another Kenyan irony, a few decades later a Black person of

Kenyan origin would become the president of the United States (and some would question his American-ness).

My colonial generation didn't know Bombay; it had aspired to London's educational opportunities, if not exactly the fairytale streets of Dick Whittington; all roads from the British colonies led there, from Accra and Lagos, Nairobi and Dar es Salaam, Hong Kong and Kuala Lumpur. But at the same time, with our strong communal identities, we had no intention of going *permanently* to London and losing ourselves in an "immoral" society. England was the place to go for prestige and training. That prestige was coin cashable only at home, in East Africa. But with the new politics of independence, "home," for so long unquestioned, had just become precarious.

Into the second year of Tanzania's independence—when my mother and many others had handed in their British passports— a terrifying event occurred in our region, and it seemed as if the predictions of the pessimists among us, that East Africa would go the violent way of Congo, had come true. Early one morning news spread in our neighbourhoods that a bloody revolution had taken place overnight in Zanzibar. Sleepy old Jangbar, as we had always thought of it on the mainland, where nothing much happened; it was where my maternal grandparents had arrived as young immigrants before moving to the mainland for better prospects. But now Zanzibar radio came out with fearful, uncharacteristic invective and threats against "imperialists." People came out on our street, looked around. Everything looked the same but our world had just changed. As stories emerged from Zanzibar of killings and rapes, prayer sessions began in mosques, jamat khanas, and temples. Was this the legacy the stout British Empire had left us? The England of the Queen, of Shakespeare and Newton, of Sir Winston Churchill (not to say the pop singers Cliff Richard and Helen Shapiro)? Our communities were for the most part ahistorical in outlook and politically naive. In retrospect, the revolution, or at least a regime change, in Zanzibar was inevitable.

In the nineteenth century the island had been the major slave market of the region. The Omani Arabs who had ruled there had maintained a racist hierarchy with pure Arabs at the top, the Black descendants of slaves at the bottom, and the Asians and mixed-races in between. (The society was described by former Sultan Barghash bin Said's sister Emily Ruete, after she had eloped with a German businessman, in her autobiography, *Memoirs of an Arabic Princess from Zanzibar*.) The elections leading to the island's independence had been rigged so as to keep the ruling class in power, with the sultan as its nominal head. The revolution occurred within days after independence.

Media speculation, threats on radio broadcast from the island, and rumours soon predicted imminent revolutions in the three mainland countries, Tanganyika, Kenya, and Uganda. Refugees arrived by sea with stories of killings and looting, news came of teenage Asian girls being pursued for marriage by elderly African revolutionaries. They dared not refuse. (A good friend of mine was married off quickly as a teenager when a proposal came from an elderly revolutionary.) Two boys joined our class in school, both soon nicknamed "Unguja"— Zanzibari. But within months, a miracle occurred. Tanganyika and Zanzibar joined to form the United Republic of Tanzania, and the "Cuba of Africa" (as the newspapers in the West had dubbed our island neighbour) was therefore reined in. In fact, Cubans had been seen on the island, and, according to some sources, Che Guevara had secretly passed through Dar after an unsuccessful sojourn in Congo. But if Zanzibar was reined in, it pulled the mainland to the left. China, the Soviet Union, and East Germany became friends, the West became an adversary. African Socialism became the national ideology. It was idealistic, but in its practice it threatened Asian small businesses and questioned "bourgeois" ideas such as placing value on academic education. But this was our home, we would adapt to change and there were ways to get around bureaucratic excesses. Young people were enthusiastic about the new egalitarian ideology, and there were already two influential Asian cabinet ministers in government.

Our British headmaster, Mr. Greenshaw, was eventually replaced by a Black African, Mr. Palangyo, a strict, somewhat troubled man who had no qualms about inflicting the cane even on the girls' backsides for their misdemeanours; but in keeping with the tradition of a British-style high school, he took pride in school achievements, be it a prize in dramatics or at a science fair or a win at a sport. He cared especially for African literature and brought several writers to speak to us (among them, memorably, Chinua Achebe). He also wrote a novel, *Dying in the Sun*, published in 1969 in the well-known African Writers Series, whose editor was Achebe. He was replaced by a Party appointee, who showed little interest in his job and appeared mainly to sit in his office reading the government socialist newspaper. When I was admitted to MIT in the United States, in response to the university's congratulatory letter to the school, this new headmaster replied—without my knowledge—that I would not be attending. America was the enemy then.

(The young people, especially those who had been to high school, and more especially the Asians, did not take the government rhetoric too seriously, though we would have agreed with its foreign policy of non-alignment. *Time* and *Newsweek* still brought us world news. We were, in short, a confused, colonial bunch.)

I left for the United States somewhat furtively, via Nairobi—where I went by bus—fearing to the last moment that I would be stopped by immigration. And yet I had always intended to return. Even after eight years and a doctorate, when my close friends were already in Toronto, I was applying for jobs back home.

As a student in Cambridge, Massachusetts, when asked, I would proudly declare, I am from Tanzania, even if the telephone operator could not distinguish Tanzania from Tasmania. To Indian students who asked, "Are you from India?" I would reply haughtily, "No, I am from Tanzania!" The US was a friendlier country then, and I had gone for the mildest of reasons, to study what I wished and see the world, see America, and return. But in my absence, the world I had left, for which I would have substituted no other, despite the excesses of socialism, shifted again. In Uganda, Idi Amin, who had appeared in a coup a few years earlier in what seemed like comical relief, came out with a racist revelation from Allah: Expel those "engineers of corruption," the Asians. Almost overnight, the Asians of Uganda were chased out of their homes and looted by the army, and became refugees, begging for a country to take them.[5] Many spent months or years in refugee camps before finding new homes, mainly in Canada, the United States, and Britain. Those in neighbouring Kenya and Tanzania felt even more insecure than before.

The three countries had always been different. President Nyerere of Tanzania was an enlightened leader. He had declared the principle of equal citizenship, not race-based Africanism. The country was stable. Still, a rumour began to stir; a whisper went around; a movement began. *We should leave before it's too late.* And those who a couple of years before had been advised to go out of their way to be Africans began to apply to go to Canada. Many went. Nobody I know has an inkling of how this happened. Perhaps—my bias—the leadership, with wealth already in deposit in London banks, decided to abandon ship and take the others with them. In the US, where I had become more idealistic, the rug had been pulled away from my feet. Friends and family began arriving in Canada.

I went to Canada on a two-year postdoctoral fellowship, still with dreams of returning to Tanzania, but soon got entangled in professional and domestic concerns, worried about security and employment. Canada was friendly, a sweet enticement to keep on staying. Yes, there was racism; I see no need to list the many casual slights and haughty receptions that were the lot of non-white immigrants. There were the homeless on the streets outside my apartment building to remind me that the place had its own problems. But there were many like me and our numbers were growing. Here, I could write, bring my world onto the page. Uhuru Street of Dar es Salaam, where I grew up, is scored through my earlier work. Here, in Toronto especially, there was freedom and encouragement, there was certainty. We saw the country changing before our eyes, and we played a part in that change.

Becoming a Canadian citizen, and relinquishing my Tanzanian citizenship, as my mother had her British passport—was a wrenching experience. One did so, one told oneself, to be able to travel freely; to arrive at a border flashing an African passport was to be treated like a thief or beggar. East Africa continues to live in me through memory, my visits back, and my always rooting for it. I know that it has been the same for many, as the messages on chat groups during the Covid pandemic demonstrated. One dare not say that loudly, for the "Canadians" resent this double face: how can you like someplace else when you live in "the best country in the world"? It is not easy for them to understand that one can genuinely have two loves. Divorcing one, even if only officially, and there seems little choice, leaves a hole in the heart.

7

Am I a Canadian Writer?

One is tempted to say it doesn't matter. Art is art, it needs no label or brand. You write because you must, not to raise a flag or beat a drum. Alone with yourself, you bare your soul, and that's who you are. To which I answer, But that is simplistic; you need to be read, you need to be seen, or you don't exist. You are an unseen star in an unseen galaxy; a hypothesis, a possibility.

To elaborate my question, I ask myself, You are a Canadian citizen, a novelist living and recognized in Canada, but are you a *Canadian* novelist? To which I respond, But what is a Canadian novel?

The answer would have been obvious once—Lucy Maud Montgomery, Margaret Laurence, Robertson Davies would come to mind. Their novels are historically, quintessentially Canadian, produced from the soil where the ground turns white every winter and the leaves turn colour in the fall. And the call from England or Wales or Scotland is audible. In today's parlance, and with history under revision, these might be called "white Canadian" works now, or Canadian Settler works. Whatever one calls them, their authenticity as Canadian can hardly be questioned.

Similarly so, now, for works by Indigenous Canadians and those African Canadians who have lived on this soil for generations. Besides recognizing its neglected peoples and certain ignored facets of its past, the country has also changed in other ways, is changing rapidly all the time, adding more people and more cultures, stirring up a multitude of ideas and interests that are often conflicting. To look for an essence, therefore, a core, a singular notion of Canadian-ness within the maelstrom is surely to try and grasp at an illusion. One is reminded of the fable of the three blind men who encounter an elephant: each man puts his hand on a part of the animal—an ear, a leg, a tusk—and concludes that it defines the whole. Or think of Zeno's arrow: no sooner have you put your finger on it than it has moved on.

As the nation, so the novel, you would think. There's no longer an essence or a trait that defines a Canadian novel. And yet some novels are regarded more Canadian than others, which are welcomed into the pantheon more like foreign guests. It is still possible to be told, When will you write a novel about Canada? Or, This novel is your most Canadian. Or even to be asked point-blank, Do you consider yourself a Canadian? Painful questions for the author, but honestly meant, asked by "real" Canadians. I've encountered all three during my tours. Not long ago a few literary critics, anxious to defend the purity of Canada's national literature, came out with their calipers to adjudge the Canadian-ness of foreign-born authors like me who had arrived recently in large numbers and wrote about elsewhere and were receiving attention in the metropolises. And had the temerity to win prizes as Canadian authors.

The cultural world, though liberal and even radical in many ways, is otherwise notably conservative and self-preserving.

However, the question I have posed—Am I a Canadian writer?—is not my plea for inclusion; I ask it—to play the devil's advocate—of myself.

In those dark moments of self-doubt that come periodically to visit any writer, those of us whose world came apart during their lifetimes—into the past and the future, "here" and "there"—and who consequently often bear the weight of an undesired hyphen or an extra description or label—are sometimes called upon to ask ourselves, Whom do you write for? Who is your audience? Where do you fit in? And even: Who cares?—what do you have to say that is relevant to this nation, to the world raging around you in all its complexity and tumult? You could have become a doctor and saved lives, an engineer and built roads. As you are, you come from the fringes of world affairs and now live in a small country as a so-called minority. Who will read you, after your adieu? What trace will you leave behind? If you're read at all, where and as what? In a Canada where you sputter out in frustration, *I am no more ethnic than you are,* I am not a professional multiculturalist, a token, an "of-colour" fulfilling a diversity quota, a tick-mark on forms demonstrating Canada's liberalism and goodness? Where you assert, I am not an immigrant writer, my writing is not immigrant, it emerges out of my being, my experiences, my knowledge? Where—be honest—a new generation edges you out, ever current with the times and angst-free, for whom there is no "there" but only "here," no loss but only gain? Perhaps, you comfort yourself, there will be a corner of recognition for you in the country you left behind, which occupies an indelible place in your heart; but are you any more relevant over there? Who *are* you now? Where do you belong?

Traditionally, a new Canadian or American—an immigrant—was someone who departed the shores of his native country, set foot on the new soil, and kissed the earth; the old life was behind him, to be forgotten. At least, let's assume this for the time being (forgetting the special privilege of those who arrived from Western Europe and Great Britain and maintained at least a cultural continuity with their homeland). Succeeding generations of immigrants adapted, spoke the language and idiom, played baseball or hockey or football. We know they were not completely integrated, often living in their own neighbourhoods—for example, Irish, Italian, and Greek—and identified by certain characteristics. They bore the brunt of discrimination, but that was par for the course. This is the traditional model of immigration, as neat as a theorem and as comforting, lending to the sociology of immigration a veneer of mathematical sophistication.

Canadian literature, correspondingly, would be characterized in this traditional picture by something essentially Canadian, revealing the existential nature of this northern nation; you might think of the theme of survival à la Atwood; you might think of nature—the cold, the wilderness, the Prairie, the mountains, the Atlantic; you might think of a certain, privileged kind of colonial inheritance that is manifest, for example, in the celebration of Victoria Day and the presence of the Union Jack as an emblem on provincial flags. There is the Prairie-grandmother novel; the growing-up-in-the-Maritimes novel; the World War I novel; the cool-thirty-something or forty-something Vancouverite novel. These are all accepted Canadian themes, to which presumably the new Canadians would adapt or add even if it took a generation or two.

Recently in Canada, however, this picture of cultural assimilation has been softened by immigrants arriving from Asia, Africa, the Caribbean, the Near East, and elsewhere. Canada is a self-proclaimed multicultural nation. It has devoted government departments to promote this idea. Undeniably this policy has fostered a national attitude, albeit imperfect and not always uniformly, of cultural and racial tolerance. No longer does a woman wearing a sari feel nervous in the streets; a Sikh can proudly wear his turban and kirpan in public; the halal sign is recognizable and the hijab is just about accepted; it is all right to be heard speaking in your native language. (This does not prevent some nut from attacking you for making yourself so obviously different.) Racism exists, no doubt, but to a much lesser degree and is less overtly threatening.

And yet, isn't this multicultural space, which we may define as allowing people to be as different or exotic as they wish, simply a waiting post, a holding area for immigrants, a quarantine to hold the alien virus and keep the peace while succeeding generations have time to emerge fully integrated and assimilated? Tolerance aside, what a joy to behold a young Canadian of Asian or African background speaking an accepted

Canadian English dialect (which the aficionado might detect as West Coast or Albertan, small-town Ontarian, or Italian or Punjabi Canadian); and how irritating, the contentious parents who claim their version of English is as good, if not better, who follow cricket but not hockey, and disappear to Chandigarh or Porto in the winter. How nice to see Sikhs discussing hockey, an African Canadian playing in the NHL and good at it! And how annoying those Asians who gang together on campuses, oblivious of everyone else. Who belongs to multiculturalism except the new immigrants, those whose mother tongue is not English and who have not quite grasped mainstream idioms and ways and can therefore be only half-formed Canadians?

In the same vein one may interrogate the significance of a novel that is set in India or Africa, for example, and is hailed—for the present—as Canadian and even receives a national prize. Does that novel say anything about Canada? Anything about its history, its politics, its societal concerns, its character and psychology; its landscape? Or does it, after all, belong to that space of the half-formed, in a perpetual winter of discontent? How will future generations of Canadians relate to it?

It is legally correct to say that a novel by a Canadian citizen is a Canadian novel, no argument. A book by a Kenyan writer who has never set foot in Canada is not a Canadian novel. This citizenship test is a safe criterion, it gives us an outer limit, tells us at least what cannot be called Canadian. But are three or five years, after which one stands before a judge, swears loyalty to the Queen (now King), and obtains a piece of paper and a card, enough to automatically produce a Canadian sensibility, a work of literature that can be called Canadian? Can an artistic sensibility be naturalized, given a new passport, in a mere five years?

It can be argued that any work of fiction or poetry produced in Canada is different in spirit from a similarly themed work written elsewhere; say a novel set in Bombay about a family crisis regarding inheritance. But is that difference significant enough or is it slight and incidental? What does it take, how many years of naturalized citizenship, to produce that significant difference, a Canadian trademark? If in the future some critic were to examine Canadian literature of the past, would they consider Rohinton Mistry, whose work is set almost entirely in Bombay, or Harold Sonny Ladoo, whose work is set in Guyana, to take real examples, as Canadian writers? If they trawled through the works of these novelists, would they bring out nuggets or essences of Canadian-ness? Will they think of Ann-Marie Macdonald or Margaret Atwood in the same vein? Don't we think of Gabriel Garcia Marquez as Colombian, James Joyce and Samuel Beckett as Irish? Was Vladimir Nabokov really an American writer? And do we really think of Joseph Conrad as authentically English? The Poles have claimed him wholeheartedly. And so, whom are we fooling with our generous, inclusive definitions of Canadian literature? Are they not merely convenient and all too temporary—while we wait for the one-hundred-percenters, the children of these immigrants to grow up and relate truly Canadian experiences, born from the soil?

A young writer of Chinese descent declared to me once how fed up he was of stories of ghosts and bound feet and Chinatown; he was impatient to tell Canada and the world his own notion of Chinese Canadian-ness—dominating mothers, conflicts between the sexes, pressure to excel, gender politics.

Not long ago, whenever I passed through Toronto's Thorncliffe Park neighbourhood, pulsating with new life, the mosques, the kabab shops, the supermarkets, the girls in hijab, the boys playing cricket, boys and girls emerging from the schools or cashiering in the supermarket, I would think enviously about the stories hatching there. They would assert a new Canada. Stories such as those told in previous decades by Mordecai Richler, grandson of Jewish immigrants, memorializing St. Urbain Street, Montreal, and Maxine Hong Kingston writing about California. At such moments, watching a new world take shape before my eyes, contemplating the literature that would inevitably emerge from the minds of some of these kids, and realizing more and more that that other world across the ocean that was similarly mine is no longer retrievable, I wonder if I have a home, as I thought I had, as I like to think I have every morning that I wake up.

The boys and girls I watched not long ago in the "immigrant" suburbs have grown up. They write stories inspired by their lives in their modest neighbourhoods of densely packed high-rises or the quiet suburbs of new houses and neat, treeless front lawns. In a recent collection of poetry and fiction called *Feel Ways*,[1] young authors from diverse backgrounds proudly claim a part of Toronto—Scarborough—mainly inhabited by new Canadians and long disdained as "Scarberia" by the downtown cultural snobs. Groomed in writing schools, versed in the new jargon of diversity, self-definition, and antiracism, they operate in a different ethos of collectivity, tied firmly to each other in the world of social media. Not for them the lonely artist agonizing over words and sentences. Message matters, labels matter. Inspired by the protests of Black Lives Matter, encouraged by a sudden epiphany—or guilt—in the white world that ignored their parents, they are ready to overthrow conventions, and turn history on its head. Similarly, a group of young, savvy Chinese Canadians make a claim on the generic Chinatown, its past and future, in the recent anthology *Reimagining Chinatown*.[2]

What of us then, in the face of this new generation of self-promoting revolutionaries? We had our time and we learned to let time take its inevitable course into today.

For writers of my ilk, I return to the statement I dismissed at the beginning of this chapter—but at a grazing angle this time and with some acquired wisdom. For me to go on writing, it should not matter how I am viewed, where I belong. I cannot pick up the pen or laptop, I cannot honestly call myself a writer of fiction if I consciously strive to demonstrate in my writing my credentials as a Canadian or African, a Muslim, Hindu, or Sikh, or anything in particular. Others can use labels to describe writers such as I am for their own purposes—theses, academic papers, editorials have to be written, after all—but I cannot work under the shadow of a label. It would make me want to scream for my freedom. In my generation there was often pressure—words of advice—to write a "Canadian" work in order to get accepted. Such a work was more immediate to the "Canadians," whom it moved and validated, and it got attention. But the result of succumbing (not everyone did) to such pressure resulted, I believe, in the disaster of the "multicultural" novel or poem, in which the author strives to show their Canadian-ness, using clichés and propaganda from immigration brochures and cringe-producing words of gratitude to the nation. One imagines the patronizing smiles and the tearful gratitude that greeted them. Today the "diversity" novel or poetry collection catches attention. But surely, doing your honest best is sufficient tribute and contribution? What needs to be said will get said.

What does it matter what you call me, or what posterity will take me for—if it will at all care to read me? This is what I am: I live on such and such a street, in Toronto or Winnipeg or wherever; I have lived before in other places that I could name for you; I have brought up children, I pay my taxes, contribute to a few charities, try to mow my lawn regularly. I clear the snow, though I tend to wait a little in the hope that the sun will come out and do the job for me. Here is what I can write, this is what the inspiration was, where it took me: a street in Dar es Salaam, a fishing village in Ghana, a cane plantation in Guyana, a tenement in Calcutta. And yes, a neighbourhood in Toronto or Surrey or Burnaby in BC, where people from such countries live alongside others born in Canada.

The discussion should end there, and it does for me. But once in a while one likes to play the polemical game and go further, in a way that does not matter to one's creativity but helps to address questions outside of it.

And so, one asks: Isn't there any way, then, in which I can be truly Canadian?—not out of the kindness or generosity of other Canadians—which let us admit gratefully has been there—but *essentially* Canadian, so that a person in Berlin or Tokyo, for example, or Nanaimo or Cornerbrook, two archetypically Canadian places traditionally, would look at one's work and say, Yes, of course it is Canadian! If so, we have to define a new, adulterated, and more sophisticated essence of Canada.

One might define and truly recognize a category of writing and a phenomenon called the "Canadian Postcolonial." Those writers like myself whose work could be described by this term emerged mainly from the milieus of the former British and French colonies—places that appear far away and alien; we create and tell the stories of those places and their people—many of whom belong in Canada now—that have not been told before, or did not have a ready reception in the metropolitan cultural centres of the world. We are historians and mythmakers; the witnesses. We are essentially exiles, yet our home is Canada, because home is the past and the present, as also the future. We belong to several worlds and Canada has given us a home, an audience, a hospitality, and sometimes even a warm embrace. We get a category all to ourselves because there are enough of us.

But we might go further and say that not only are there so many of us from other parts of the world, there are entire coherent communities that have settled here, possessing a common heritage and history; and we are telling their stories. They came with their clothes, and sometimes with their spices and pots and pans, and gave the writers among them the responsibility of bringing along and telling their stories. These stories are not for their nostalgia; they are their history, their myths. They validate and heal, and they anchor their lives in this new land. And the stories are for their future generations as well. I have often been stopped and thanked by people, young and old, for telling their stories. (Once, though this was in Nairobi, after my reading at the national museum, a man came over to me, visibly in tears. "Who tells our stories?" he asked. "We are the forgotten people.") Through their stories newer Canadians make connections to other Canadians, for they are human stories, after all. And that puts a whole new dimension or shade to the question of who we really are as authors.

If we are telling the stories of Canadians of so many diverse backgrounds, aren't we then telling the stories of Canada as well? What kind of Canada? A Canada not only of the Mounties and hockey, the North and Newfoundland, the corny beer commercials, into which newcomers vainly try to assimilate; but a Canada that also constantly adjusts and redefines itself. It is a Canada that is as much urban as it is the North. If eighty percent of a nation resides in its cities, then cities deserve to be recognized as emblematic of the nation, defining it as do the Rockies, the Prairies, and the Atlantic.

This idea is, naturally, anathema to many people—those whose Canada of the mind, of *their* memory and history, was imbibed in childhood and jars with the multiracial, multilingual kaleidoscopic reality churning outside their windows. Neighbourhoods and cities no longer look the same. Has the sense of our national self disappeared? they anxiously wonder.

Where has our Canada gone? We are tolerant and law-abiding, they say, we will admit that a Canadian is anyone who is a citizen. But there must be a limit. There are strong emotions involved in the idea of a changing Canada. This is not only the gripe of the folk who hark back to the Canadian Dominion or of the white supremacists who fear for their race. There is also the more sophisticated lament that goes around, that Canada, unlike America, has not created a powerful mythology, a dominant sense of itself as an entity in the world; instead, we have had to accept the notions of the wimpy underdog, the self-deprecating or numbskull but consistent and dogged Canadian, a cheerful denizen of the northern latitudes with a meagre imagination. Just when the country had woken up from American cultural dominance and begun to assert itself with its sense of itself and its literature, here came people who wrote about alien places and different histories, who polluted good old Canadian English with Swahili and Hindi idioms, making *halal* a Canadian word.

The idea I am putting forward here, against this mode of thinking, is that the story of Canada must be the story of all its peoples; and that story gets augmented and changes. The self-image of the nation evolves. Canada's past is embedded in the land itself and the stories of its Indigenous Peoples; but it also undeniably includes the stories, and indeed histories, brought by the immigrant settlers from Britain, France, and the rest of Europe, histories and thoughts that go back to the Bible and Classical Greece and Rome; to this sense of origins and the past, I claim, must be added what has been brought over from Africa,

Asia, and elsewhere. Canadians with roots in Europe fought in the two world wars, and that involvement and its stories are a part of the nation's history; but many new Canadians and their forebears have been veterans and heroes of those world wars too, and yet others have struggled heroically in other conflicts, in wars of liberation in Africa, Asia, and South America; surely these struggles must now be a part of Canada's history. Our children, however much they insist in the manner of all youth that the past does not matter, also demand this acknowledgement, that their history and ancestry belong to this land. The stories of the Jewish Holocaust, the holocaust in Rwanda, the Partition of India, the trauma of Apartheid, the Atlantic slave trade, and the massacres in Kenya and Cambodia are Canadian stories.

A hundred thousand and more new Canadians come to these shores every year; few people will say that this country has turned for the worse because of that. To remain viable as a country, we have no choice but to allow our population to grow by 0.5 to 1 percent every year. There was a time not long ago when the Rockies and the Prairies, the quaint small town and the waters and the wilds were Canada; no more—the reality has evolved. Canada now includes Don Mills, Brampton, Mississauga, Surrey, and Burnaby, all proudly vibrant with urban life, new and exciting, and full of possibilities.

In this kind of convex reality, in which the world comes in, gets refracted and reimagined through Canadian writing, there is perhaps a place for writers such as I, who will always wash upon these shores, with stories to tell.

8

Nowhere with God:
Uneasy Confessions of a Syncretist

I have often wondered and speculated about my community's—the Khoja Ismailis'—nomadic, restless heartbeat. According to folk history their wanderings began when some eight centuries ago their caste—the Lohanas—ventured south from the Afghanistan region towards Kutch and Gujarat. The Mongol invasion was rampant in Central Asia in those times. In their new homes, perhaps in the fifteenth century (dates are understandably vague in this oral history), they chose to become followers of an itinerant mystical preacher named Sadardeen, a Shia Muslim whose roots were in Persia. Now calling themselves Khojas, they gradually set themselves apart from their fellow caste members and village folk in a spiritual migration that I think of as a prequel of things to come. They had added only a gloss to their traditional beliefs in the Indian gods, but it would foretell their future existence in the following decades and centuries as they set forth into the world to places like Rangoon, Colombo, Muscat, Malindi, and Zanzibar. In the late nineteenth century my father's grandfather arrived at a small town called Kibwezi in Kenya that stood on an ancient caravan route that wended its way from the Indian Ocean coast across the interior to Lake Victoria and beyond. My father, an orphan in the custody of his maternal aunt, in his youth wandered about in Kenya and Tanganyika (and even attempted a visit to India) until a bride from Mombasa finally grounded him.

When I was about thirteen, at an idle moment between us in her shop in Dar es Salaam, my mother related to me the story of Draupadi, the virtuous wife of the five Pandava brothers of the Indian epic the Mahabharata. At the point of being violated by their evil cousins the Kauravas, who had won her at a game of dice, she beseeched the lord (Krishna) to protect her; as a result of her plea, when her sari was pulled off by the evil Kaurava, Duryodhana, another one appeared in its place, and so on, one after another. Thus she was preserved in her chastity. This story is a folk version of the one related in the great epic, but to my mother it simply demonstrated the power of faith and prayer. To me it was intriguing, evoking a magical time in far-off India, though I expressed typical teenage scepticism: How is that possible? It's possible, she said. How can five men marry one wife? They did.

Why would my mother tell me this story? A professed Hindu might object, But you are a Muslim! Likewise a diehard Muslim might say, That is a Hindu story! To which I reply, But it is *my* story, I heard it at home. Do I need to explain more? It's an Indian story and my heritage is Indian. It belongs to the Khoja tradition of Gujarat. Khoja worship for centuries centred upon the singing of hymns called ginans (from the Sanskrit *gnana*, "knowledge") in the vernacular Gujarati (and, to a lesser extent, in Sindhi), which often relate fragments from ancient Indian stories in order to instruct, inspire, and exhort. These stories are about some specific venerated characters from the Indian scriptures (or mythology, depending on one's belief), in particular Draupadi, Harishchandra, his wife Tara Rani (also known as Taramati), Anasuya, Mata Kunta (commonly called Kunti), and Yudhisthira, the oldest of the five Pandava brothers who married Draupadi. One particular ginan relates how Harishchandra and his queen, Tara Rani, sacrificed all—kingdom (Ajodha), beloved horse (hanslo), darling prince (kunvar)—for the sake of their faith. It would be sung with hair-raising devotion by our entire congregation in Dar es Salaam while standing in the jamat khana every New Year's Eve. It was the time of new appointments in the community's leadership and served to impress upon everybody the gravity of that responsibility. It was a call, like the call that came for Harishchandra and Tara Rani, and they gave. *Amar te aayo*—the call came.[1]

How can that not be *my* story?

Similarly, exasperated at my teenage arrogance my mother said once (or more than once): "Raja Ravana's pride got him nowhere; where will yours take you?" Ravana was the powerful demon of the Indian epic *Ramayana*. Mother was simply paraphrasing another of our ginans: "[With] Lanka his fort and the ocean its moat / Mighty Ravana still came to nothing."

What was I, then—Hindu or Muslim? It may sound obtuse, but the *or* in the question troubles me intensely, more so in our recent, divisive times. In my view, the question need not even be asked. Why must we choose between two poles, when we stand on neither side? And yet it comes up with an insistence.

You are a Muslim! Your name says so. But my surname, I counter, which is my grandfather's Lohana name, does not say so, and neither does his father's name, nor our clan name, the attak, which refers to the third of the five Pandava brothers, the invincible Bhim. What would you have me do with those enchanting stories that still live in me? Should they simply be allowed to vanish into the ether, transitory phenomena in the continuum of time like puffs of smoke, without leaving a trace? Why should a name foist upon me an identity, a system of belief, a sense of belonging or not belonging?

As I go about my everyday life in Toronto, most people I see don't care a fig about my beliefs—what God, gods, or goddesses, what plant, animal, or stone I worship; they may guess—usually erroneously—where I come from, but the question of religious belief doesn't arise. It's only with another brown face that this question rears up like an evil genie. People from the Indian subcontinent seem to always carry with them a bag of labels from which at any instant they will take one out and stick it on your forehead with that special eureka of discovery and (I imagine) a smirk, along with all their stereotypes. They have placed you. Hindu, Muslim, caste, subcaste. Friend, foe, neutral, vegetarian, non-vegetarian. I squirm at this assault on my privacy, on my very sense of myself.

I decided to write this confession provoked by a fellow novelist who was born in East Africa, whom I will call Rajab. We were at a conference hotel in Washington DC having a drink, when he happened to say to me, with a teasing grin: "But you are not Muslims!" Rajab's tease referred to the Khoja Ismailis, with whom he was familiar as neighbours from his childhood. On a previous occasion, I had happened to be with him and a few other writers at al-Aqsa mosque in Jerusalem. We had been allowed inside by Israeli soldiers who guarded the entrance (a more vocal and obtuse segment of our delegation had been turned away) and arrived near the spot from where, on a Ramadan night, the Prophet flew up into heaven, mounted on a horse, and had a vision of Allah. The emotion on Rajab's face as we stood there in the cavernous hall of the mosque was astonishing to see and at the same time deeply moving. "I wish my father could see me," he, whom I guessed to be an agnostic, murmured. He went down on his knees and said a prayer. But I felt nothing close to that emotion, only intellectual curiosity, and perhaps some envy, and a desire not to forget the moment and its details.

Rajab's reaction at al-Aqsa mosque was of someone who had been brought up in a tradition steeped in the life and deeds of the Prophet Muhammad. I know only a few episodes of the Prophet's life, and for me there is not quite the same emotional charge in the stories as there is for someone from that tradition. They are interesting and instructive. Some of them I've learned only recently from reading the Prophet's biographies as research. But the story of Harishchandra and Tara Rani deeply moved me; as did the vision of Draupadi. How could I not see a sister in her? Or my widowed mother in Mata Kunta?

The Khoja Ismaili prayer house was called the khano (short for jamat khana, and it was called something else in Gujarati previously) and was separate from that of the Muslims; we prayed differently, sitting on the ground, men on one side and women on the other, no partition in between, in the manner of a Sikh gurudwara. Indeed, when we spoke of Muslims we most often meant Sunnis. The inspiring stories and miracles we heard were mostly about the Ismaili imams. Were we to be asked if we were Muslims, we would say yes. We celebrated the two Eids, but we did not fast or go on hajj; most of us had never read the Quran or had even heard of the Hadiths—the deeds and sayings of the Prophet as related by oral tradition—and we were discouraged from indulging in too much meat. Only recently had our daily prayers, which had been in Kutchi and Gujarati for generations and referred to the ten avatars of Vishnu, been replaced with a few Arabic verses from the Quran.

Therefore, when Rajab said to me, half seriously, "But you are not Muslims," I surprised him by responding, "I never thought of myself as one." I tried to explain why: we came from a syncretistic tradition, our identity was communal and unique, etcetera. "Write about it," he said.

I don't believe he really cared, but I had often thought of doing exactly what he recommended, because during my lifetime I had seen that syncretistic tradition—so enchanting to me, with its odd mixtures and illogic, its magical stories, its mysticism, and its beautiful hymns, partly in old Gujarati, that we had heard and sung daily and only half understood; and humanistically satisfying though radical in accepting that diverse spiritual paths all led to that same goal of enlightenment—I had seen this tradition slowly, and then at a gallop, wilfully transformed—chipped away, erased or rewritten to remove perceived conflicts with Islam; in other words, to purify it from an Islamic point of view. To rid it of its "Hinduism." So relentless has been the process that it seemed that soon even I would forget that the tradition really existed as I remembered it. Did we really have a ceremony during celebrations at which unmarried girls arrived in a procession into the congregation, each carrying a pot on her head and led by an older woman? Or the story of the woodcutter and his mother, recited with a very particular sonorous intonation, a tremolo, on the seventh morning after new moon—when we were served sweet yellow rice with sooji halwa and boiled black channa with coconut chips? Did we have an *aarti* sung first thing as services began, again in that sonorous intonation, whose refrain—*aarti kije nikalanki taniji*—streams into my mind after decades as I write this? On the back wall of our prayer house was there actually a *takhat*, a majestic throne with ample silky cushions, where people came to offer flowers and ask for favours? Did we have in our homes, as an occasional propitiatory rite, a luncheon for exactly seven or fourteen girls, who would then leave with a little gift of a handkerchief and a sweet? Sometimes the girls' toes would ritually be washed by the hostess. My mother had a particular fondness for this tradition, called *niaani*; it helped her in difficult times. *Niaani* means "womenfolk" and was a sacred word in our family. And those thrilling recitals of ginans in the khano that we can recall with as much fondness as jazz aficionados today might recall a stint by John Coltrane or Dave Brubeck at a

New York club. I should record all this, and yet for whom would I write? The subject seems so petty and local, so unimportant in a world that is on fire everywhere.

There arises this recurring question: Does it matter, this remembering of a minor tradition, this concern about its erasure? Why not let history take its course, let the tradition shed and moult and renew itself? Species of life, tribes of people, entire languages disappear. Cities and countries are ravaged by wars. National boundaries are redrawn or invented. Millions are forced to leave their homes. Global warming threatens devastation. Robots replace us at work, and our idea of the mind may need revision. And more recently the Covid pandemic, the wildfires, and floods that have brought such a sense of doom to humanity. Why raise a cry about a nonconforming tradition from an obscure, dry part of India? Christian Europe rid itself of the Cathar and other "heretical" non-mainstream beliefs centuries ago. (Though they used the Inquisition and its tortures to implement this erasure, as depicted powerfully in, for example, Umberto Eco's *The Name of the Rose* and its film version.) But a perverse side of me, once in a while, when a beloved ginan comes to mind unprovoked, raises a protest: But it was there! It was authentic and alive like an obscure little animal—do we smother it? Let's at least acknowledge it before we gas it! Who should decide which story, song, or painting should be erased from our inheritance? Remember the Bamiyan Buddhas!

I have tried to explain the tradition to my Indian friends, only to give up in embarrassment. I could be describing Maxwell's equations of electrodynamics (so elegant in every way). The eyes glaze over, the expressions fall into a mask of blank indulgence. I am the Ancient Mariner. If I try to explain the tradition to an avowed Muslim I sense disbelief, even contempt. The very idea of syncretism is inconceivable: Aren't you a Muslim? Then how can you possibly also be a Hindu? Why would you wish to regress into a state of jahiliyya (ignorance)? Don't they worship cows?, an Iraqi Canadian literary critic said to me once, very disturbed at my disclosure (after which we lost touch).

It may sound churlish or antediluvian, and perhaps it's the wrong moment, to deny you're *exactly* a Muslim at a time in history when Muslims feel embattled and persecuted. In Canada at various times recently, women wearing hijab or niqab have been physically assaulted; the incidences may be rare now but the fear remains, they may still happen. Mosques have been attacked, not infrequently.[2] In the United States a Trump decree officially discriminated against Muslims. In India, chat groups vent extreme hatred against Muslims, who were even blamed for the spread of the Covid pandemic. Extremists there have called out for their genocide, without a demurral from the national government. (To be sure, in Islamic Pakistan, Hindus, Christians, and Ahmadiyyas have also suffered discrimination and violence.) With these reminders before me, I admit then feeling small-minded and guilty. You want to abandon a sinking ship, I tell myself. But more than a billion avowed Muslims, the majority of them youthful, do not make a sinking ship. I am not denying my real but rather tenuous historical link to Islam. I understand the angst of Muslims at the condition of their coreligionists, and their anger at the mockery of their Prophet. But I assert my cultural and historical Indianness: I am brown, I speak Indian languages, I eat Indian food, and I have these hymns in Gujarati extolling Hari (Krishna) that I was brought up with and love. They are beautiful, and haunting, and historical. Once in a while I get a craving for Bollywood. I am drawn to visiting India despite the problems I have mentioned. India keeps calling.

I have lived in North America for more than four decades and am a Westernized agnostic from Africa. My position is simply this: I am just what I am, the way I was made and have evolved. Perhaps I'm both Hindu and Muslim; or neither, *Neti Neti*, as the ancient wise men of India put it. I recall Draupadi and Harishchandra and Tara Rani, I recall the magical Narsingh avatar of Vishnu, who coincidentally, significantly, was both man and lion. I also recall the stories of Ali rescuing Muhammad at Khyber in Arabia and the martyrdom of Hussein, but these Arabian stories not with the same immediacy. They happened there, far away in the desert, they were narrated; the others were sung night after night and bred in the bone. I wake up sometimes with a ginan verse in my mouth (if it's not Beatles or Rolling Stones or some other pop song from my youth). They are me.

In Delhi I came to know a young scholar who is from a community called the Husseini Brahmins. Just the name should raise eyebrows. This community traces itself to Iraq, where apparently it assisted the Prophet's grandson, Imam Hussein, at the Battle of Karbala, where he was martyred. Following this episode they migrated across Iran to India, from where they presumably had originated. It's an exhilarating story, precious as a rare gem; an example of natural human diversity and creativity to hold against the forces of divisiveness, the orthodoxies and fundamentalisms that have been editing and purifying our thoughts and beliefs and imaginations. Uniformity should be subverted. My community, the Khojas, I thought proudly, had done that.

There is, above all, that joy in syncretism, the intellectual flexibility and nurturing of curiosity, the tolerance or acceptance of other ways of belief, the inability to hate others "just because." As I write this, in Delhi, I recall a friend telling me two days ago, beaming with pleasure, about the memorial service to his cousin that he had just attended, where a vocal group had recited songs of Kabir, the fifteenth-century mystical devotee who also was neither Hindu nor Muslim, equating Ram and Rahim. Hindus and Muslims have claimed him. When he died, it is said, his body vanished and in its place inside a hut were found some rose petals, so that his followers would not squabble and fight over what rites to perform.

I take here a little space to describe, briefly and simplistically, the syncretistic tradition of the Khojas of Gujarat and East Africa as I knew it during my growing up. The reader unfamiliar with Indian religious mythology may easily skip this section. In describing this tradition, I speak not of a great civilization and great conquests and cultural and intellectual achievements—I have no claim to that boast, though my modest background equips me to respect individual genius wherever it sprouts on this planet. I speak of a folk tradition—villagers in western Gujarat imagining stories and creating meanings about life and death and the universe around them, drawing from cultural veins going down to the hoary past, away from the eyes of the rajas and sultans, the pandits and mullahs—those guardians of orthodoxy, assassins of the imagination.

The Khoja beliefs are founded on the basis of the teachings of the itinerant preacher or guru called Pir Sadardeen (whom I have introduced above) and a few of his descendants, some few (perhaps four to six) centuries ago. The tradition blended the Indian devotional practice called bhakti, based on the worship of the god Krishna, the mysticism of the canonical Bhagavad Gita and the Upanishads, analogous concepts from the devotional and mystical Islam of the Sufis, and medieval Ismaili esotericism from Persia. Bhakti was widespread in medieval India, its teachers and gurus—Mirabai, Narsinh Mehta, Kabir, Guru Nanak, and many, many others—singing hymns (called bhajans) as they travelled about from place to place gathering followers in much the same way as Pir Sadardeen and his descendants did in Gujarat; Khoja hymns were called ginans, their vocabulary often identical with those of the bhakti bhajans. The Khoja faith, in combining these traditions, equated Krishna (Hari) to Ali; the god Brahma to Prophet Muhammad; and the

Quran to the Atharva Veda (the fourth Veda). Interestingly, the god Shiva and the Mother Goddess hardly if ever appear, which is surely a subject for a dissertation or two. The equivalences however are entirely superficial, and crude, and point to a people who were not learned in the canonical scriptures. To the Khoja villager in Gujarat, hardly aware of what kind of world and peoples lay beyond his domain, the name "Ali" would have conjured up nothing more than the familiar blue god Hari (Krishna). In fact "Hari" occurs many more times in the ginans than "Ali." This mischievous flute-playing demon-slayer's stories suffused the very air they breathed, his images were ubiquitous throughout the land, his deeds were celebrated in the wonderfully colourful festivals like Holi and Navratri. The Khoja villager would have had no access to either the Arabic Quran or the Vedic-Sanskritic Vedas and Upanishads. He would have had no knowledge of the Islamic traditions that thrived in the centres of the north, such as Delhi, Agra, and Lahore, and beyond in Persia and the Middle East, expressed in Persian and Arabic. (In a shrine to Pir Sadardeen's grandson, Imamshah, outside Ahmedabad, there is a place where pilgrims on their way to Ganga [the River Ganges] would sit and meditate and when they opened their eyes they would realize that they had just visited the holy river.)

There are some fascinating, recurrent patterns (besides the absence of Shiva and the Goddess) in the ginans that lend them a coherence, telling us that they are not simply arbitrary syncretistic occurrences, there is some thought and construction behind them. For example, we find only certain characters from

Indian religious mythology in them: Kunti, in the unusual form of "Mata (Mother) Kunta"; Draupadi, also sometimes occurring with "Mata" or the respectful "ji"; Prahlada as "Pehelaj"; and Yudhisthira as "Jujesthana." All these are introduced as exemplars of the faithful devotee. Yudhisthira's presence is specially intriguing. In the epic Mahabharata, he is the eldest of the five Pandava brothers (and son of Kunti), a valorous fighter but not as great as his two younger brothers, Arjuna and Bhim. Arjuna is the hero, the skilled archer close to Krishna, who is his charioteer and guide during the epic battles. Bhim is reckless and indestructible, such is his physical strength. Neither can be found in the ginans as I know them. Yudhisthira, on the other hand, in the epic is shown as noble and righteous; it is he to whom the others defer and who feels pangs of guilt at the destruction that has been wreaked by the war and therefore needs to be consoled. It is he who tries to bring peace even before the battles begin, ready to give up his leadership for its sake, who finds no satisfaction but only grief in his side's ultimate victory. And it is he, in the vernacular (Prakrit) form Jujesthana, who appears in the Khoja ginans as embodying virtue. Prahlada (Pahelai) is another faithful hero. Harishchandra and Tara Rani, as mentioned before, recur in the ginans, and their kingdom is Ajodha Nagari (Ayodhya). Surely there's no point in discussing whether it is the same as the contentious present-day city of that name in the state of Uttar Pradesh, the site of so much modern-day contention and cause of bloodshed.

Pir Sadardeen sometimes signed his compositions as Guru Sahdev and Satguru. Sahdev is the name of one of the two younger Pandava brothers, born to Pandu's younger wife Madri, and legend says that Pir Sadardeen had visited Varanasi (Benares) on the Ganges, presumably to learn from or debate the learned pandits there. Almost all the ginans begin with the call "E-ji!"—a respectful form of "O Sir/Madam!" The tenth avatar of Vishnu, who would arrive from a land called Sehentara Dvipa, is often referred to as sami-rajo (swami raja), the lord-king. Krishna recurs as Karsan, Vaikuntha Nath (lord of Vaikunth, his kingdom), tribhovara sami (lord of the three worlds) and, most of all, Hari. The faithful Khojas or devotees are referred to as momana-bhai, "momana" being the vernacular form of the Arabic or Persian word for "follower," and "bhai" the Gujarati for "brother." Munivara, meaning "good seeker of truth" (from the Sanskrit *muni*), rikhisara (from *rishi*), meaning approximately the same, and virabhai also occur frequently. *Vira* is "hero," also used by Kabir.

There are some long compositions, including the intriguing Twelve Books, one of which is titled Nakalanki Gita ("The Song of the Pure One," i.e., the tenth avatar); another ends its lines with the suffix "-am," in mock Sanskrit. (I have found a Sikh composition using the same convention.) I never heard them sung. One long ginan, consisting of some four hundred quatrains, is called "To Munivara Bhai" ("And so my good seekers") and begins with how Vishnu, with the aid of the goddess of learning, Saraswati, and Brahma, created the universe and how it evolved.

The Khojas even had their own writing script, apparently to keep their scriptures secret, called Khojki. (It was common among Indian communities in the past to possess their own jealous variations of the Nagari script, upon which the present canonical Hindi script is based.) But it is unclear (to me) if all the compositions were actually authored by the holy men to whom they are attributed; they could be community efforts developed over several centuries. Some were no doubt part of the folk oral tradition of Gujarat. (I have found verses from one beautiful little ginan on an LP recording of Gujarati hymns; on the wall of the factory making the legendary patola cloth in the ancient city of Patan, Gujarat; and on the wall of a shrine just outside Vadodara.) Undoubtedly over the centuries they underwent alterations in language, and we expect there to have been interpolations. I have two copies of "To Munivara Bhai," mentioned above, that I translated once when I seriously considered pursuing a higher degree on a study of the ginans and the culture in which they emerged. One of them has an extra verse at the end; and there are verses in the middle, obviously the work of a pious meddler, admonishing against the consumption of tobacco! The ginans that we have now in print were collected in the late nineteenth century by one Lalji Devraj, and they must have gone through a selection process. No doubt the selection must bear Lalji Bhai's stamp. Different Khoja communities across Gujarat might have preserved their own favoured ginans. But there is a consistency to the corpus, a thought process or vision, as I've said, working against the meddlers. Today's meddlers, fearing the wrath of Islamic fundamentalists, have substituted Ali for Hari and Mowla for Sami (Swami)—an example of the travesties inspired by modern Indo-Pak politics and jingoism.

The Khoja religion is, then, a syncretism embedded in the Indian folk milieu, specifically that of Gujarat. It partakes of stories and beliefs that have existed and evolved for over two millennia on the Indian soil, using them to form a distinct philosophy of belief. It has been around from three to five hundred years, though some claim for it a thousand years. The earliest one or two teachers, ancestors of Pir Sadardeen, supposedly came from Alamut, the Assassin Ismaili fortress in Persia. When it was destroyed by the Mongols in 1256 CE, Orthodox Islam celebrated. This then is the Khojas' link to Islam. (There is a chronological conundrum to this supposition, a gap between the eleventh and fifteenth centuries to explain.)[3]

The Gujarati Khoja tradition has been perceived as a mongrel, a half-formed, impure faith that given time and coaching will eventually drift to authentic Islam or Hinduism. It defies easy description, violates census classifications, and does not have the clarity that scholars of the neat and canonical wish to study. And yet it is authentic in itself, having preserved itself and evolved over the centuries, during which it has defined a historical community. In India similar communities have always existed and they are the targets of religious purifiers to this day. We often forget that the canonical, mainstream "pure" forms of any religion as we know them are themselves artificial constructs, they did not arise fully formed.

True, the Khoja tradition is not refined. It has contradictions. The ginans have the ragas but not the sophisticated meters of classical poetry. Some are philosophical, others devotional or mystical, yet others didactic, and some seem trivial ("When you come to pray, virabhai, join your hands . . ."). But the corpus is inspiring and intriguing, its material authentic—several hundred verses plus the Twelve Books with an identifiable character. In the face of modern times it needs interpretation and study at the very least, and perhaps room to evolve or be turned to music, but it does not deserve burial or the flames. The beauty of its poetry and music, its sheer creativity, need to be held close and nourished, not bound in the iron claws of Orthodoxy and Ideology. Anything refined and pure is hard to digest; it can be poison. We have seen enough examples of fundamentalism and nationalism in our times, and their results writ in blood.

Nevertheless, aspiring to a perceived modernism and craving legitimacy, the Khoja community's leadership has seen fit to transform it, rhetorically at least, into a pure Islamic sect, with all the chest-thumping gusto of a new convert. This is not the place to go into the mechanics of this self-transformation. That would be too controversial. But the net result has been the quiet removal of "Hindu" practices, and the shelving of many ginans or verses, accompanied by a loud drumbeat of Islamic rhetoric and a sly occlusion of Gujarati origins in favour of imagined Iranian and Central Asian ones. Not surprisingly, some young Khojas now grow up in North America with the belief that their ancestors came from Iran or Tajikistan. And "scholars," with no knowledge of an Indian language or of Indian anthropology and folk history, knowing a smattering of Arabic from university courses, with no poetry in their souls and little imagination go about picking nuggets of Islam in these wonderfully vibrant, mysterious and evocative songs of a people.[4] The Khojas are today a much-admired community, successful in many fields including politics, business, and journalism, but they are highly susceptible to authority: if they were told the ginans were composed by a goat, many would be likely to believe it.

Does it matter? We were a small, outlying community from outlying districts of India and Africa; why not conveniently become extinct as one and define ourselves as another, possessed with a glorious past in which "we" had a named empire (Fatimid, in Egypt), made conquests, and showed intellectual prowess—and in a short time no one would be the wiser? This new self-identity would be, moreover, most conducive to life in North America, where origins matter less than in other places: in the New World, "dynasties" can spring up instantly. When two easy and clean orthodox paths (Hindu and Muslim) are available, why choose the thicket in the middle? Moreover an Islamic identity is easy to define and explain—it has the simplicity of geometry: beginning with the birth of the Prophet it goes down to the present, with only a few branch lines to take you to your particular sect. Say the shahada, the statement of belief, and you have it. (Though the simpler the definitions, the sharper and more threatening the edges, the more glaring and sometimes bloody the differences.)

And the Islamic identity looks attractive: doesn't it feel better to belong to a global fraternity—the umma—with a recorded history of glorious achievements, rather than to a folkloric, humble past in rural drought-stricken Kathiyawad, India? Don't we all create mythologies, imagined and embellished beginnings, personal as well as national? Memory, in any case, as the neuroscientists tell us, is constantly renewed.

You have a problem if your truth matters: memory nags. We speak of the bane of fake news. Do we simply acquiesce to fake history? Accept fake identity?

How to avoid that twinge of cynicism or stab of irritation at seeing a young Canadian with India and Africa in his blood struggle to cough out Arabic gutturals while attempting to recite authentically a Quranic verse that he doesn't understand; when an Afghan is brought to a wedding merely to recite the Arabic nikaa (with the proper gutturals), after which he departs, and the guests fall back into English and Kutchi and some pick up their glasses of wine; when young people resort to Arabic calligraphy as an art form, ignoring their Indian and African heritage, their Western education?

We rightfully celebrate human achievements anywhere. As someone trained in theoretical physics, I have been excited by the achievements of Einstein and Dirac, Bose and Ramanujan, Weinberg and Salam, and many others. My first sight of Picasso's *Guernica* in Madrid was soul-stirring. Hearing T. S. Eliot in his recorded voice was intensely moving; so was hearing (and meeting) Faiz Ahmed Faiz. But what should make the tenth-century Fatimid Empire of Egypt occupy a special pride of place in my heart? A thin and vague sectarian connection through a maze of controversial history?

I see in the community in which I was brought up a desperate need to belong to something great, to be validated; that's understandable in any small and previously colonized group that sees itself as otherwise insignificant. But will borrowed glory and questionable connection to a distant history satisfy that need? When you erase your own tradition and history, or rewrite or invent them (and it is done casually, just like that), at the end of the day you are left with nothing that is deeply felt. The Persian new year Navruz becomes an acquired habit; the Arabic prayer becomes a formula recited by rote; Arabic calligraphy is the new, heartless art form; a Tajik dance becomes yours; a Saudi king gives your child his name. Can art and history, can culture be so easy and superficial?

In colonial times, it was amusing to see black and brown men and women affecting English accents, the men outfitted in pinstriped woollen suits even in sweltering heat. But the Khoja mimicry that I've mentioned is more than a bunch of innocent, transient fads, it is a systematic erasure and invention. Still, why should this bother? It need not, of course; but half-truths, inventions, and ignorance have a way of nagging when they negate your own experience and memory; when they negate your own history. There is an ideology to the mimicry. Essentially, as I see it, the requirement has been to become shorn of heritage and ancestry; of mystery, ritual, and song; of memory and traditions; of culture; in short, to be deracinated, and onto that plain slate that emerges to transpose an "Islamic" tradition and culture that are fictions. I can only say, No, thank you, to that. I will keep my memories and move on; I have evolved from them, as is natural, but I do not want to negate them. They belong to times that have shaped me. Some of our ways were narrow-minded, ignorant, and superstitious; others had ancient roots, they brought meanings from ancient times, they gave us belonging in ourselves, in where we came from, and in where we lived.

But that leaves me at the bus stop, neither here nor there; or more precisely, nowhere.

Respect, even belief in the other faith, is not unknown to India. It is, to many of us, its "beauty" and strength, its attraction, a source of pride. The seventeenth-century Mughal emperor Akbar had a Christian, a Muslim, and a Hindu wife, for each of whom he had separate quarters and prayer rooms. The late president of India, Abdul Kalam, was a professed Muslim who fasted during Ramadan and prayed the namaz (Muslim prayer); he was also a vegetarian, read the Gita, learned Sanskrit, and had a spiritual guru. Holy places and saints in India have often had followers from all faiths. The shrine of Sabarimala in Kerala attracts millions of pilgrims every year, who arrive from long distances, often on foot and dressed in black dhotis; the last approach to the shrine is a climb up a steep hill. Before paying obeisance to the god of the shrine, a form of Krishna, pilgrims first pay their respects at a nearby shrine of a Muslim saint called Vavar. The Kali temple of the Pavagadh pilgrimage site in Gujarat was topped with a Muslim shrine and a mausoleum to a Sufi, Sadan Shah. (It was under threat during the 2003 communal violence. Another ode to modern politics.) The fifteenth-century mystic Kabir, whose songs are popular to this day, is beloved to Hindus, Muslims, Sikhs, and many in the West. The twentieth-century saint Sai Baba of Shirdi, whose images adorn rickshaws and middle-class homes, is believed by many to have been a Muslim; whether he was or not, his teachings combine elements of both faiths. And finally, bringing this observation to a full circle, the shrine of the grandson, Imamshah, of the Khoja Pir Sadardeen lies a short distance away from Ahmedabad, at a place called Pirana, in Gujarat. It is visited by people of all faiths and at its head sits a Hindu guru. Ginan books were on sale when I visited, though I recognized none of the ginans in them. (However, a reverse erasure had taken place here: during my latest visit, Imamshah was now said to have been an orphan, born to a Brahmin couple and adopted by Muslims. But as a Khoja "cousin," I was made very welcome there and given pride of place to sit.)

Muslims are a "minority" in India because at independence diverse sects and castes, including the "Untouchables," were brought together under one "Hindu" umbrella to make up the "majority." Thereby Muslims and Christians became the "minorities." This is absurd: majorities and minorities are invented concepts. Many Dalits—the so-called Untouchables—detest the Hindu scriptures, which sanction untouchability and even violence against them. Hindus and Muslims of the Punjab and

Sindh provinces, for example, are often more related to each other than to the populations of Bengal and Kerala. There can be few examples of such absurdity more glaring than the definition of former Pakistan, consisting of Punjabi-dominated West Pakistan and Bengali-dominated East Pakistan. The latter broke away in a violent nationalist struggle to form the new nation of Bangladesh. Its national anthem: "Amar Sonar Bangla" (My Golden Bengal), its lyrics written by Rabindranath Tagore.

And yet, despite such hallelujahs to eclectic practices and syncretistic beliefs in India, the actual attitudes that have come to prevail in the country in recent times, and not only among the fundamentalists, are essentialist and emphasize difference—and, more and more, hatred and enmity—rather than unity. Muslims and Hindus seem to inhabit different universes. Hindu liberals will speak up for "minority" rights, but their social lives will remain almost entirely devoid of Muslims. Muslim causes are a hobby or simply lend left-wing respectability, and they can be offensively patronizing. Housing in India remains segregated, and stereotypes abound. I am often exhorted to eat meat; it has come to seem that for me to be vegetarian in India is to encroach upon a precious upper-caste Hindu identity.

In the *Indian Express* not long ago (March of 2018), Harsh Mander, a human rights activist, observed that "open expressions of hatred and bigotry against Muslims have become the new normal, from schools to universities, workplaces to living rooms," and concluded, in April of that same year, that "India has never been as divided since Partition . . . The poisons of hate have penetrated too deeply into our souls." The columnist Tavleen Singh came up with an even more scathing observation.[5]

Perhaps, then, there's no choice for those in between, and the Khojas are right to have moved away from their Indian roots to an invented, new identity? Their cousins, those who possess the shrine at Pirana, have moved in the opposite direction, towards a pure Hinduism. What's not true, when repeated often enough, becomes the new truth.

Writing this confession comes with its risk. Not that I expect a fatwa pronouncing a death sentence, or to be physically assaulted where I live. There is, however, the other type of risk, that of opprobrium from your own tribe—people you have grown up, played, and gone to school with. A community that's family and, perhaps partly by necessity, peaceful. But the smaller you are the more threatened you feel. You've always balanced between two extremes or orthodoxies, two definitions, with the risk of offending purists bearing either label. Your tenets sound odd to those who follow the established formulas of orthodoxy. You are exotic or a heretic. You call yourself esoteric. In modern times you need respectability and recognition, for which you have accepted the need to redefine yourself. But you need time. And so every revelation or confession is perceived as a betrayal. In Nausari in Gujarat there is a shrine to another holy man sacred to Khoja Ismailis; it is also worshipped by a community of the Patel (Hindu) subcaste. At a very modest temple nearby,

I saw a book of ginans lying open on a podium. Remarkably, it was printed in the same format I had seen in many ginan books of my childhood. The place was empty, except for the priest hovering inside. Explaining myself (of course he had heard of Khojas), I asked him, Do you sing the ginans? He said, But we have to be careful.

Is it necessary or even ethical, then, to stand out and make such revelations as I have done here? Why not let time take its course, let the community approach a philosophic ground, one more congenial to where it wants to be in the modern world? My position however is not meant to be disruptive or, in the vein of *Charlie Hebdo*, "I will say it because I am free to say it." I do so with trepidation and with apology. My purpose is simply to record certain phenomena in the life of the community in which I grew up, traditions, practices, songs, and rituals that nurtured me, to say that they indeed were there, this is how it was; and to call out the deliberate erasure and re-invention of its culture and identity by ignorant leadership, without due regard even for keeping records or seeking consensus—or indeed being honest.[6]

9

Gandhi: Discovery and Reappraisal

1.

On January 13, 1948 Mahatma Gandhi undertook a "fast unto death."[1] This was to be his final fast, and perhaps he had a premonition of that. Gandhi was seventy-eight and a grieving man. India had achieved its freedom, after a long, mostly non-violent struggle, but at a cost few would have anticipated. The nation that had been India had been divided into two rivals, "India" and "Pakistan," in an acrimonious partition that was the cause of unimaginable misery, as millions crossed the new borders and horrifying violence rampaged across the affected areas. Perhaps non-violence had been an illusion, after all? Gandhi was in Delhi, having arrived at the capital after bringing peace to Calcutta; he had accomplished for Bengal—it was said—what a border force of 55,000 men was failing to achieve towards the west, in Punjab. His presence itself had already brought respite to Delhi; nevertheless, the resultant calm in the city was more the chill of a terrible apprehension. Hindu refugees from Pakistan had flooded in, bearing stories of rape and murder; consequently, the Muslims of Delhi lived in fear of reprisals. Gandhi was a man of action; he had led many non-violent campaigns in the past, but he now felt helpless against this overwhelming madness. As his last resort against the almost imminent nightmare in Delhi, he undertook the fast. "Death for me would be a glorious deliverance rather than that I should be a helpless witness to destruction of India, Hinduism, Sikhism, and Islam."

A withered old man lies in foetal position on a cot on the porch of a wealthy supporter's bungalow home, his body covered in a white cloth. His eyes are closed as an endless queue of people, rich and poor, powerful and humble, file past him, some openly weeping, others offering prayers. His weight is stable at 107 pounds, doctors worry about his heart. The prime minister of the new nation—the Harrow- and Cambridge-educated, sophisticated and charming-when-he-could-be Jawaharlal Nehru—comes by to visit, and cries. Finally, on the fifth day, leaders from across the city, including the chief of police, stand before him and sign a pledge to guarantee the peace. It is a stirring moment. Not many days later, walking out of that house to lead a communal prayer in the front garden, he is shot to death by a right-wing extremist from a group claiming that he had appeased the Muslims.

Who was Gandhi? Was such a man real, as we conjure him up in our minds—a self-sacrificing saint of peace with a heart large enough to bear compassion for all of humanity? Is he relevant anymore? India's recent achievements, political, economic, and technological, can hardly be said to have followed a Gandhian path. Why then does Gandhi continue to inspire and move, not only Indians but others as well? Perhaps there exists in us an innate desire to believe in pure goodness, that impossible ideal that he seemed to embody, for which his people gave him the title of mahatma, "great soul." Perhaps in our horrifically violent world—but when was it not so?—we dream of a deliverer to cleanse it in some climactic or epic moment.

A voluminous and ever-growing literature exists concerning Gandhi; indeed an industry in his name churns along. He himself wrote copiously, giving his views and explaining his thoughts to fellow Indians. He began his *Autobiography* in Gujarati in 1925, when he was fifty-six. (Its Gujarati title, *Atmakatha*, is more eloquent: "soul story.")[2] Translated into English and revised for the popular 1940 edition, it is fluent and engaging, and remarkably intimate and candid. It is our best source about his childhood and early life. It was my introduction to Gandhi.

My discovery of Gandhi was quite accidental. I had seen photos of him as a boy. He seemed laughable then, a diminutive, wrinkled man in a dhoti. This fact is embarrassing to admit. It reflects both the arrogance of youth and a state of ignorance, in a colonial culture in which to wear a tie was a sign of civilization and sophistication, and in a religious-ethnic community whose spiritual leader was the be-all and end-all of existence.

How often has it been said that you have to leave home in order to discover yourself? For my university education I went to the United States. One day, while idly walking through the aisles of the annual college book sale, I happened to pick up—quite arbitrarily—a book by Jawaharlal Nehru. It was his autobiography, and cost a dollar—an affordable risk for an indigent student. It was the first book written by an Indian that I read and

I found it fascinating and moving. It was also the first Indian voice I had heard from afar—barring the films, of course, which were fantasy. It was a charming voice about a privileged childhood and youth, vastly different from what mine had been, but that tale of self-discovery immediately spoke to me. Through it I became aware of India's own independence struggle, and I learned about Gandhi, about whom Nehru wrote,

> this little man of poor physique had something like steel in him, something rocklike that did not yield to physical powers, however great they might be. And in spite of his unimpressive features, his loincloth and bare body, there was a royalty and a kingliness in him which compelled a willing obeisance from others.[3]

My world had begun to shift its axis. I had unearthed a hidden vein in my life-being.

A year later, in an elective course on psychoanalysis and history, a combination that perfectly addressed my concerns about who I was, I read Erik Erikson's book *Gandhi's Truth*. In Dar es Salaam when I was growing up, there was no commemorative M. G. (Mahatma Gandhi) Road, as there is in every city in India, there were no statues of Gandhi; my elders might have known of India's independence struggle, I didn't. I knew of Africa's struggles, in Kenya, Tanzania, South Africa, Zimbabwe, Angola, and Mozambique—which were immediate and rousing. My extensive reading was also entirely in English; my education was in science. Now due to this fortunate circumstance of a liberal arts requirement in my university curriculum, I was reading about Gandhi, a Gujarati like myself—or more properly, like my grandparents—who had lived in England and Africa, who had held the world spellbound. In a chapter titled "A Personal Word," Erikson, a Swedish American psychoanalyst, addresses Gandhi directly, respectfully, apologetically. He says,

> Mahatmaji,
> As far as I can gauge it, I am now about midway through this book and as eager as any of my readers to follow you to India and to that period of your life which was shared by my witnesses. But first I must say a word . . . [4]

Imagine the reaction of a twenty-year-old fresh from a colonial backwater, awed by everything he saw around him in America. From that backwater India had seemed even more backward and poor. I was impressed. I could imagine the white-haired Swede, a Harvard professor, sitting at Gandhi's feet, pleading. *Mahatmaji, forgive me but I have a problem.* Erikson, a student of Anna Freud, was a man of eminent stature. His bestselling book, *Identity: Youth and Crisis*, addressing the problems of the day in America, was widely discussed. For such a man to address Gandhi in a respectful, apologetic manner, the way a student would address a master, I found overwhelming. (Most people today, of course, haven't heard of Erikson.)

I proceeded to read Gandhi's autobiography in its English translation. In my enthusiasm, moreover, I also ordered several copies in the original Gujarati from a new friend who was visiting India. I found the Gujarati version hard going, my Gujarati being domestic and rudimentary, and I didn't finish it.

My discovery of Nehru and Gandhi coincided with—or further impelled—my own affirmation of my Indian-ness, during a time of my own struggles abroad. I was African, yet also Indian. I came from a community few had heard of. It was the early 1970s and the Western world was in a state of upheaval. Every day, in America, news came of yet more deaths in Vietnam. The threat of nuclear annihilation loomed (except perhaps to policy makers, but the radio regularly announced rehearsal warnings of nuclear attack). South Africa was under apartheid rule, Zimbabwe (then Rhodesia) was ruled by a white minority, and in the US the Black Power movement was in full swing. All around me, young people had arisen in defiance, challenging not only the premise of the war in progress abroad but also the premise of the privileged lives they had lived and the future they had been taught to expect.

Whatever one thinks of those times, analytically, cynically, or in hindsight—and that depends on the background one came from—for someone like me it was impossible not to be swept up in the youthful wave of exuberant challenge, defiance, and searching. It was an exciting time, a thrilling time, and a scary time. What was on offer, expressed in all forms of media—film and television, books and pamphlets, teach-ins and public lectures, songs and drugs—were revolutionary, life-changing alternatives—to morality, to politics, to lifestyles and worldviews. I had come from a place where authority was respected, government was feared, public opinion curtailed, and social conformity bred in the bone. I had been brought up in a small community in a small city; like the world before Copernicus, it had been the centre of the universe. Now my world I saw as a backwater like the furthest small planet, a Pluto in the solar system, and my worldview had been shattered in what I have come to see as my rebirth. Suddenly, now, I had to think for myself, learn about myself, make up my own mind about the issues of the day.

Gandhi, searching for his own "truth," talking about his own struggles abroad, was therefore immensely attractive. He was an exemplar. He gave me the courage to find my own truth in place of the ready-made one I had come with—with all its safeguards and warnings against deviation. When I arrived in the United States, I was terrified of deviating from that righteous path (as I thought of it). I agonized about it. I even composed a letter to myself, to be opened in the future, warning myself not to deviate, and if I had done so already, then to quickly return to the straight path. That letter remained in my mind, was never written.

Over the years, in a cosmopolitan university, in a city brimming with intellectuals, in a tumultuous time, I developed an eclectic worldview—so much was on offer, in terms of the new and exciting science I learned, the spiritual gurus who came by, the psychologists and activists who spoke. Whereas I had been brought up on school curricula designed for success in the professions, and a religious worldview that was narrowly communitarian, I could now read the Gita and the Upanishads, and be mesmerized by a Sufi song, or a poem in English, or a bhajan of Mirabai, a devotional song by the Beatle George Harrison, a film by Satyajit Ray or Ousmane Sembene. I could read Freud and Jung, Russell and Popper, Sartre and Camus, Lenin and Marx.

Mohandas Gandhi in particular attracted me with his courageous self-inquiry and his honesty. That he was an Indian and a Gujarati was a bonus. He spoke my language. But there was an essential point where I differed from Gandhi. Gandhi believed in a God, he died with God's name on his lips—*He Ram!* When he was in foreign lands, God came to his aid. It was God who helped him remain a vegetarian in England. Who saved him from the temptations of lust.

But God had walked away from me.

Here was a man who led mass movements for human rights and dignity, who has been credited with bringing independence to India; a man who walked into the bullet of an assassin for believing what he did, crying out for peace and mutual understanding. He was heroic. But great as he was, Gandhi was human. This is often forgotten by his worshipful followers. His attraction for me has always remained personal—as I discovered him—as a man struggling with himself to be true. A man who till his last breath had doubts.

There were always the personal costs and moral risks of his journey. Gandhi's struggles for moral purity, for one thing, pushed aside or ignored the needs and desires of his immediate family. It was always *his* experiments with truth, by which his wife, Kasturba, had to abide, and the demands of which his children had to follow. When he went to London as a young man, he missed his mother terribly. "My mother's love always haunted me," he tells us. But he says nothing about missing his wife. When he was sorely tempted by "lust," it was God who saved him, not his guilt about possibly betraying his wife. In South Africa, when he "freed himself from the shackles of lust," taking a vow of celibacy, walking on a sword's edge of temptation thereafter, we don't know what Kasturba felt before she came around to his decision. Once, however, in an argument regarding the cleaning of chamberpots, she told him, "Keep your house to yourself and let me go!" Of course she didn't go.[5] (Where could an Indian wife of that time go?) Gandhi calls this a lover's quarrel, adding, "But I was a cruelly kind husband. I regarded myself as her teacher . . ." This cruel kindness may seem fitting for the time, but the modern observer balks. It is about this attitude that Erikson chides Gandhi, saying, Wasn't your love simply an excuse to exercise your will?

A bitter and prolonged private tragedy in Gandhi's life was the fate of his eldest son, Harilal, who had joined his father in the Satyagraha movement in South Africa, spending time in prison as a result, but later broke away from Gandhi, resentful of his treatment. He went on to become a Muslim, reverted to Hinduism, and ultimately died an alcoholic. During his later years, in India, he would see his mother but refused to see his father. His life has been captured in a moving film, *Gandhi, My Father* (2007).

Gandhi's struggles with his "lust," while he lived a celibate life, led to one of the most controversial and, to his followers at the time, distressful episodes in the final years of his life, when he would invite young women to share his bed to test his chastity. This behaviour was shocking even to his most ardent followers at the time. You have to be a real believer in his super-humanity to excuse this behaviour, and there are those who do. But by and large the modern sensibility would chide the old man, saying, This is not done, sir; think of the lives of the girls—they are not there for you to prove yourself.

One might argue that ultimately a man has his own con-science—or inner voice—to answer to, not a collective one. In the last resort he cannot but be self-centred. But surely we expect that inner voice to guide us to be heedful of others around us and how we treat them? Love and devotion demand—or the inner voice demands for them—empathy and compas-sion. Gandhi was a leader; he fought against the misery of millions in his homeland. But in the process he became insen-sitive to those who were immediately around him or he put them to the most stringent tests. The rest of us mortals, who do not have the multitudes counting on us, see the tortoise point of view.

There is a feature of Gandhi's own religious background that very often and, to my mind, significantly, if not deliberately, seems to be simply ignored. Gandhi says in his *Autobiography* that he learned about Hinduism when he was in London as a young man. This was at the time when he came under the influence of the Theosophists. What he learned, naturally, was the canonical Hinduism of the Brahmins and scholars, and one cannot but wonder if this was not where he first thought of Hinduism in its purity and oneness. Anything in its pure form we know excludes others; it is what we call fundamentalism.

Gandhi's own religious upbringing was, however, far from the canonical or Brahminic. (He was from the Bania—Vaisya—caste.) He was deeply influenced by his mother Putlibai, to whom he was devoted. She came from a small Gujarati Vaishnava (Vishnu-worshipping) sect called the Pranamiya. As one scholar, Uma Majmudar, observes,

> Putliba brought her own maidenhood heritage of the Pranami faith (a sect of Hinduism) to enrich the Vaishnava heritage of her in-laws' family. Prannath (1618–1694), the scholarly founder of this faith, established close scriptural-theological links between the *Bhagavata Purana* of Vaisnavism and the *Quran* of the Islamic faith ... According to Stephen Hay ... "the Pranami sect was noted for its latitudinarianism toward Islamic ideas and social contact with Muslims. One of the distinctive features of the Pranami sect was that it worshipped no images of deities." As Gandhi recalled, there were no deities in the *Pranami mandir* (temple); what he saw instead on the walls were big, lively pictures and beautifully inscribed passages from both the *Bhagavata* and the *Quran*, which made a lasting impression on his child mind.[6]

An article in the *Times of India* describes a Pranami festival under the title, "Where Krishna Meets Muhammad," beginning as follows:

> Tulsaben Thakkar takes Prophet Mohammed's name as she recites from a Hindu text. She talks of qayamat [Judgement Day in Islam] while singing praises of Lord Krishna. It is a daily ritual for about 60 lakh followers of the Hindu Hijanand sect, now popularly known as Pranami, founded 400 years ago in Jamnagar, Gujarat. Their love for Krishna also invokes the holy Prophet.[7]

Books on Gandhi, if they care to mention this background, fail to give it due significance, which is remarkable, when it could be used as an example of the unity of all faiths and to pull people together. One presumes that it would be too embarrassing to dwell on this detail, which does not quite fit in with the rising view of the nation as essentially Hindu, or the politics that led to Partition, or the hatred that has gradually welled up in sections of Indian society. But right up to modern times (though in decreasing numbers, for obvious reasons) communities have existed that did not make clean divisions between the two faiths. In my own travels through Gujarat, I have observed this phenomenon in different settings.[8]

2.

The reappraisal. I must present a caveat here. Gandhi lived a long and active life. He wrote voluminously. Surely he must be allowed to alter or develop his views, contradict himself, become dated, have an off moment or make an error. Moreover, Gandhi studies is an endless tangle of views, counterviews, and always some more, which I have never had intention to negotiate. My critique or reservation here must be seen in that light. It is as personal as the way I discovered the man, the mahatma.

The Gandhi who returned from South Africa in 1915 was already a potent political force, a leader of people who had organized and led mass campaigns against an oppressive government. He was world-famous. Arriving in India with much fanfare, he almost automatically became the totem, the leader, and the inspiration in the struggle for independence. But in his leadership of a country with a multitude of contradictions and opposing forces, pitted against an obstinate empire, he had to be pragmatic and limited in his activism to achieve his goals. It is now that the moral force—for me—weakens, or compromises itself. Politics and pragmatism exact a toll.

I come to my position, this reappraisal, having lived long in a secular society where my faith, whatever its nature, is my private concern. Not so in India, where you're identified with it—whether you like it or not—as though it were branded onto your forehead. I have been to India many times since my discovery of Gandhi; I have seen it as my ancestral and spiritual homeland, while at the same time witnessing the deep divisions between Hindus and Muslims, between the castes, and (to a lesser degree) between the north and the south. The hostility between India and Pakistan, created in the Partition of India following independence, continues. I have been horrified by the sheer savagery and the hatred that periodically well up during the country's so-called communal riots. And I cannot help but ask, could not the moral force that was the Mahatma have cut through the Hindu-Muslim division and seen them as one, as the same people? Did he, if not enhance, then entrench this tragic division? There have been other saintly figures in India, such as Kabir and Sai Baba Shirdi, as mentioned before, who were blind to the divide, seeing the difference as superficial and only the human spirit as real.

Gandhi's position on Muslims and Hindus is not one that I, as a person living today, can accept. Instead of seeing the two religious systems as existing in varieties and shades, including syncretistic ones that borrowed from, adapted to, and grew from either faith, and therefore belong to both—which his own upbringing must have taught him, as I will discuss later—he followed the orthodoxies and accepted Hinduism and Islam as two fundamentally separate, immiscible structures, and the followers of each to be *essentially* different from the other. All mystics will tell you, on the other hand, that they are essentially the same. Gandhi allowed the purifiers of Islam and Hinduism to raise their walls even higher. Most Muslims' roots in India run as deep as those of their neighbours. Often they come from the same castes, bear the same last names. Gandhi ignored all other differences—caste, class, linguistic, ethnic, and cultural—but not this one, the inflammation of which over the years has caused in the end the greatest injury to the subcontinent.

We know that historically the term *Hindu*, derived from the name of the River Indus, was used to describe the people of India and not a single, monolithic religious group.[9] The beauty of Indian-ness, as many people still attest, has been its diversity and embracing nature. In those tumultuous times of the early twentieth century, when so much was at stake in a divided country, the divisions between Hindus and Muslims were enlarged and exaggerated for political and pragmatic ends. Yet Gandhi was the Mahatma; we expect—or perhaps it's safe to say I expected from my distant vantage point—more from him. I expected him to have attempted to bridge that gap. Instead, while believing strongly in the sanctity of all religious beliefs, even believing that they prayed to the same God, he was also carried away in the tide of the "we-Hindu" position. Hence my disappointment in my beloved, youthful myth.

I can imagine my younger self asking, echoing Erikson, When you said "we Hindus," Mahatmaji, whom exactly did you mean? Would you have excluded me from that fraternity?—I, who do not make a distinction between them, who believe in our common humanity? When I went to India, that division and these labels were hurled at me, in spite of myself. And you, Ji, would have gone along with that?

All this sounds naive, and admittedly it makes me foreign. I am outdated, and happily so. My Indian friends return a blank look when I mention the simple fact that my ethnicity and my ancestral roots supersede the faith into which I was born—which in any case was syncretistic. We all have differences, what makes me so fundamentally different from them? I am as different from a Kashmiri Muslim as I am from a Tamil Brahmin. The implied answer is, You have to be one or the other. Can't I be both? I see shudders. If that position offends, can't

I be neither? Can't I simply *be*? A "Person of Indian Origin," as the Indian government officially designates me? Over the years since independence, the Hindu-Muslim positions have hardened; the Muslims have become "purer"; and the Hindus, aided by an artificially created majority status, have turned their faith national. Bollywood blithely portrays this fact, so that even Muslim actors play the roles only of Hindu characters. And I, who come from a local tradition in Gujarat in which Allah was merely Vishnu, and now believing religious faith to be irrelevant or a private affair, have to dodge the labels flung at me.

Gandhi's position on the Dalits—members of the "Untouchable" castes, whom he called Harijans, "children of God"—has been divisive and controversial. Gandhi desired desperately that the Dalits remain a constituent part of that constructed monolith, the Hindus, which would make them a large majority dominated by the historically privileged castes, while relegating everyone else to the status of protected but surely patronized "minorities."

Gandhi said he loved Harijans: ". . . it is my aspiration to be born a Bhangi in my next birth."

> The position that I really long for is that of the Bhangi. How sacred is this work of cleanliness! . . . I respect, I adore, both of them [Bhangi and Brahmin]. If either of the two disappears from Hinduism, Hinduism itself would disappear.[10]

Note his concern for "Hinduism."

Caste distinctions, which are eternal in India, should be kept, he said; they are essential, with the proviso that the mistreatment of the Dalits was abhorrent. He spoke and wrote strongly about it. His compassion and empathy can never be denied. He even called himself an Untouchable. But that is precious. What exactly does it mean? Merely cleaning a toilet does not make you an Untouchable. That distinction comes from being born to your Untouchable parents, who received that status from their own Untouchable parents, and so on, in an inheritance of outcaste-ness and contempt going back for generations and centuries. What does the Untouchable want? The answer is that the Dalit does not want to be patronized. Dalit life-stories, belonging now to a genre of Indian literature, depict horrific oppression at the hands of the upper castes,[11] occurring right up to recent times, and even today if media reports are to be believed. Ill-treatment of Dalits is moreover sanctioned by some of the scriptures. Consequently, modern-day Dalits have vehemently attacked the scriptures and many have become Buddhists. But Gandhi wanted all forgiven under an idealistic new majority "Hinduism."

Columbia-educated Babasaheb Ambedkar, a Dalit, was highly suspicious of Gandhi's positions on the Dalits. The two had a long-standing issue on Dalit representation in the independent Indian government. In 1956 Ambedkar became a Buddhist. Now for every Gandhi statue in India—in the north at least—there is an Ambedkar statue, because the Dalits, still the "lower" and "backward" castes, are a political force.

Finally, racism. Our iconoclastic age relishes bringing past heroes down regardless of context. No doubt this has been justified in some cases. Gandhi, for his part, has somewhat gleefully and anachronistically been called a racist recently for his attitude towards Black people.[12] For the statue-topplers, he is simply too high, too good to be true. But of course he was not a saint, as I have already pointed out above—there were no sacred omens at the birth of the child Mohandas in Porbandar, Putlibai gave a normal birth. And so not surprisingly, more than a hundred years ago he carried the biases of his people and brought them with him to South Africa (where he went in 1893 as a young man of twenty-three).

But Gandhi's constant self-doubt and -interrogation could not but bring him around. As American antiracist activist Lynn Burnett writes,

> Indeed, in Gandhi's early career, he fought for the rights of the Indian community in South Africa partly by arguing that Indians—with their history of building great civilizations—should not be subjected to the same laws as "uncivilized" Africans . . . [Yet] he would soon be arguing that what was truly uncivilized was to degrade those who engaged in physical labor . . . and to refuse to engage in such labor oneself, although happily reaping the fruits of it.[13]

Gandhi, in South Africa, went on to be deeply affected by the Black civil rights struggle in the United States; he was influenced in particular by Booker T. Washington, about whom he wrote an article in 1903. In turn, the American Black activists, including W. E. B. Du Bois and Marcus Garvey, paid close attention to Gandhi's struggles.[14] In 1926, Burnett tells us, Gandhi wrote an article titled "Race Arrogance," in which he denounced "the injustice that is being daily perpetrated against the Negro in the United States of America in the name of and for the sake of maintaining white superiority."[15] Later, during the Second World War, he wrote to President Roosevelt that "his claim to fight for freedom and democracy was preposterous, given that Black Americans were denied both."[16]

The Black Americans, in particular Du Bois, did not all agree that Gandhi's methods would work in the US (until Martin Luther King arrived). But Du Bois respected Gandhi and the two would exchange letters. In one of his letters to Du Bois, Gandhi wrote,

> Let not the 12 million Negroes be ashamed of the fact that they are the grandchildren of slaves. There is no dishonour in being slaves. There is dishonour in being a slave-owner. But let us not think of honour or dishonour in connection with the past. Let us realize that the future is with those who would be truthful, pure and loving. For, as the old wise men have said, truth ever is, untruth never was. Love alone binds and truth and love accrue only to the truly humble.[17]

And so the case against the Mahatma is not so simple. But the industry churns on.

3.

Is Gandhi relevant to the world today? India is a divided and largely a militarized nuclear nation; communalism and violence especially against women and children are widespread; the Dalits, Gandhi's so-called Harijans, favour Ambedkar over Gandhi; India's greatest and now much-admired cultural export, namely modern Bollywood, appeals often to sex, violence, and alcohol. In the rest of the world, too, terrorism and state violence are on the increase. And economic wisdom everywhere favours ever more consumption and possession. "Growth" is the mantra. In the modern world, the Indian middle class is a consuming juggernaut.

Gandhi himself sensed his failure and irrelevance towards the end of his life. A disappointed man, he observed India's Independence Day while fasting in Calcutta. "I am a back number," he said. "No one listens to me." But today he is undoubtedly still the great moral and spiritual exemplar of our times, a man who open-eyed and with breathtaking sincerity spoke of Truth in a manner few people could without being labelled as cranks, and pursued it with heroic pertinacity. Gandhi's personal Truth may inspire, but has few true followers. Gandhi's ideas for the governance of India had been rejected even before independence. In Calcutta once, when a scientist asked him what people like him should do if the new India ordered them to develop nuclear weapons, he advised, "Resist them unto death." Today India and Pakistan both possess substantial nuclear arsenals and immense armies poised for war.

At the level of human rights, however, Gandhiism as non-violent action on behalf of the oppressed has worldwide adherents: we only have to think of the civil rights activism of Martin Luther King and Cesar Chavez in the United States, the Solidarity movement in Poland, the freedom movements in Africa. In India, furthermore, Gandhi's name is still a prompt to conscience, his shadow looms perpetually over any public discussion of poverty, the ills of the caste system, the rights of minorities, and violations of the environment. (Gandhi's photo above the judge's bench in Bollywood court dramas may look hypocritical, but surely serves as a useful admonition.) And everywhere in the world, as we witness global disasters one after another, and as we become more aware of our treatment of animals and the environment, we might pause to think if human needs need reconsideration, even a little, along Gandhian lines.

10

The Urge to Get Away: Finding India

In 1325, at the age of twenty-one, "swayed by an overmastering impulse," as he later recounted, a young man called Ibn Battuta set off from Tangier, Morocco for a pilgrimage to Mecca, on the way traversing the countries of North Africa. Such was the thrill of the journey that after his hajj he kept going, reaching home in Morocco twenty-four years later, having travelled to East and West Africa, India and China, over sea and land. In all he journeyed 73,000 miles and produced an account, *The Rihla: A Masterpiece to Those Who Contemplate the Wonders of Cities and the Marvels of Travelling*.[1] There have been many other sojourners in the past who hold one in awe. Al-Biruni, a scientist and mathematician from Central Asia, visited India several times over a period of thirteen years beginning 1017 and produced an account of social observation that is still in print today.[2] Between 627 and 645, the Chinese Buddhist monk Xuanzang had journeyed in the opposite direction, to Central Asia and India, reaching as far west as Samarkand and Bamiyan (making note of the statues that in 2001 would be destroyed by the Taliban) and as far south in India as Gujarat, Maharashtra, and Tamil Nadu. His observations are recounted in

The Great Tang Dynasty Record of the Western Regions,[3] which inspired the sixteenth-century Chinese comic novel *Journey to the West*, of which several English translations are in print today.[4] In 1269 Marco Polo the Venetian embarked on a journey that took him on the Silk Road all the way to Beijing where ruled the legendary Kublai Khan, grandson of Chinggis Khan. These and other journeys of the past were slow, difficult, and tedious, and always full of dangers. These travellers produced wonderfully detailed accounts of the places they visited that fascinate us even today. (In later centuries there were of course the exploitative and aggressive European journeys to South America and Africa that led the way to their colonization.)

Whence the urge to travel?—the need to leave the safety and comfort of a home, the habits and routines and the intimacy of the hearth, and set off lonely for some distant place, uncomfortable and alien? Is the enticement the destination or the journey itself? Is it the curiosity to see the new and foreign or the need to discover oneself—that person deep inside that's been calling? Is it the need to let go and renew oneself? A physical journey has often been used as a metaphor for a spiritual quest; such were some of the hymns of my childhood. "O Traveller, what do you bring back?" A woman waits at the door, anxious for her beloved's return, a longing reflected in the term *viraha*.

Since early childhood, much as I have always longed for home, and much as I am a creature of habit, I've also had an irresistible urge to go away somewhere. My first journey was at age four and a half, when my mother, newly widowed, moved from Nairobi to Dar es Salaam, where her mother and siblings now lived, having moved from Mombasa. It was a long journey, and there was much luggage in the manner of that time, my mother having packed most of our household furniture. We went by train to Mombasa first, then by ship to Dar. Much later, in my second year of high school, when a notice arrived in class calling for two volunteers willing to transfer to a school in Iringa, a few hundred miles upcountry in the southwest where I knew nobody, my hand shot up. No thought of the family, to which I was devoted, or the friends I would leave behind. (The headmaster rejected my offer to go.) I would not say that the impulse came from my innate love of travel exactly, because I always get anxious before I set out. The urge was perhaps to experience the new and alien, to get away, to escape the rut. I would attribute it to a centuries-old itch in my people to set forth for the unknown. (I have described my family's journeys briefly in chapters 6 and 8 of this book.)

My first momentous journey happened when I finished high school, when I was sent for my National Service to a military farming camp outside Bukoba, a town on Lake Victoria, at the far northwestern end of the country. I knew nobody there and nothing about it besides its name. I had tried hard to have my assignation moved to a place closer to home, but in vain. I remember arriving in Bukoba late in the night after a gruelling twelve-hour journey by bus following twenty-four hours on a slow train from Dar es Salaam. Having got off, I lay nervously in the bed of a hotel room, waiting for morning to arrive, when I would have to make my way somehow to the camp. I was in a strange town, a naive and pious Asian teenager, and there were only Africans all around. I had lived among them but not with them. This was the first time I had stayed in a hotel, and there was a raucous bar below my room. When morning came, an army Land Rover, to which I was directed, transported me and my metal trunk to the camp, which was in a forest area by a stream. The unwieldy black trunk, filled with clothes and foodstuff, was completely unnecessary, as I soon found out. In subsequent weeks, I spent Sundays on leave in the town, where an Asian family, unknown to me previously, hosted me, providing me with fresh Indian food, a bed to take a nap, and a hot bath. Afterwards I would be driven to a highway junction to walk back to camp on an eerily silent, dark jungle track, fearful of any crack of a branch or crick from an insect, or any lurking forest spirit that might walk out from among the shadows of the giant trees on either side of me. The few months I spent in National Service, away from home, living a rough and rudimentary life with comrades of different African and Asian backgrounds, turned out to be some of my most memorable and rewarding. They were a gift and opened my innocent eyes to Africa and the world.

Shortly after my National Service, I left for university in Cambridge, Massachusetts. For the next eight years I would be on the train whenever possible, visiting new friends who were also students from East Africa, in various college cities along the northeastern corridor. A pocket-size Amtrak schedule was a fixture in my wallet, and railway stations became familiar places. I completed my graduate studies in Philadelphia and proceeded for my postdoctoral work at Chalk River, Ontario, another far-off, unknown place.

To me, Canada was, as to most Americans, in the back of beyond, to the north. Chalk River, I had imagined, lay close to the Arctic Circle. It wasn't quite that, but it was small and isolated, beautifully quaint and by the Ottawa River, temperatures falling to minus 40 Celsius. Most scientists and engineers lived ten miles further away in Deep River. In the winter some of them skied to work (one Scotsman rode a bicycle) and weather was a favourite topic of conversation. When a colleague, himself from England, asked me during my first days there how I was faring in my new home, I said I felt like David Livingstone in Africa. That raised an eyebrow. After Boston, New York, and Philadelphia, this was a major change in surroundings. It was beautiful but lonely. I learned (painfully) to ski cross-country. Some weekends I would go to Montreal by bus to be with friends and meet my fiancé, a girl from Dar whom I had met in Boston, who would have hitched a ride from there; on my return trip at night I would be amazed at mothers tearfully bidding goodbye to their children who were travelling only as far as North Bay. I would be dropped off on the highway at 3 a.m. and walk back like an alien into a dead town of suburban houses and beautifully lit streets.

I relocated to Toronto two years later, and finally with a sinking feeling moved with my young family into a house. Was I now to remain rooted in one place forever? But it turned out that I had many opportunities to travel, including visits back to East Africa. In Canada I have travelled with my family by road and train from the Atlantic to the Pacific. My most significant journey, however, occurred in 1993, when I visited India for the first time.

THE URGE TO GET AWAY

—

Travelling solo, out of the familiar—in a train racing through a vast flatland or along the edge of a mountain ridge, at an airport in the midst of anonymous throngs, on a bus on a road on a dark night illuminated only by a single pair of headlights—you gaze wide-eyed and in wonder. You realize your minuteness. You are but an atom existent in the infinite diversity of the earth, a dot in the long passage of human history, a speck of consciousness in the flow of Time. You realize the insignificance of the individual, the errors of the preconceived. These precious moments are to hold close when you fall back to the mundane. The young Flaubert during his visit to Egypt in 1849–50 was moved enough by what he saw to write, "the Orient ... flattens out all the little worldly vanities. The sight of so many ruins destroys any desire to build shanties; all this ancient dust makes one indifferent to fame. At the present moment I see no reason whatever (even from a literary point of view) to do anything to get myself talked about. To live in Paris, to publish ... all that seems very tiresome from this distance."[5]

India. A fellow from Dar whom I met in Toronto told me once that when he first set foot on that ancestral homeland, he kissed the ground. What potential charm it held in the imagination, what potential embrace. How different it has become. How conflicting yet unbreakable that tie to it.[6]

I arrived in India already with a sense of the momentousness of the occasion; India was not just any exotic place; it was *the* place, the ancestral homeland. It was not just a visit that I made, it was *the* visit. As soon as I set foot on the airport carpet in Delhi and joined the queues, I found myself observing keenly and anxiously, attempting to relate what I saw to what I knew—or thought I knew from what I had heard and read and seen in numerous films since my college days of discovery. As I looked around me I wanted, needed everything to reflect the specialness, the uniqueness of this extraordinary arrival. I also knew that I was an outsider, though privileged by my ancestry, and my perspectives would be from a distance. But the experience that unfolded over the days was totally unexpected, it was overwhelmingly one of immersion and engagement. Soon I did not know who was "them" and who "I." India was a maze from which I could not turn back. It was a mirror I looked at to find myself, and entered, and never completely returned. If I thought that being a Canadian and a Tanzanian African born in Kenya were conflicting enough, with all its guilts and uncertainties, here was another dimension to myself, a third corner to my identity. I had thought India had lain dormant in my consciousness, but here it was, very much alive and asking in its turn: Who are you, really?

How does one write about such a visit? Is there anything really special about the experience? North Americans of European ancestry have been visiting Europe for over two centuries; if we go by accounts, this does not lead to an emotional depth charge, a deep soul-searching, an interrogation of identity. While there is an affinity, a cultural, political, and racial identification, differences are evident and have been examined in many films and novels, for example in the fiction of Henry James.

African Americans have had a special affinity for Africa, manifested strongly in the mid-twentieth century in visits to the continent by eminent personalities such as Malcolm X and Stokely Carmichael, and Alex Haley's reconstruction of his slave origins in the hugely popular book *Roots*. Africans from the continent too have made the connection, for example in their adulation of Muhammad Ali and Barack Obama, and in the exchange of popular culture. West Africans recognize a tie with the Blacks of the Americas due to the volume of the Atlantic slave trade. The Nigerian writer and Nobelist Wole Soyinka relates in the second volume of his memoirs how he discovered a remnant of his Yoruba culture in a settlement in Jamaica, and a village in Brazil with distinct memories of its Yoruba roots. Similarly, the Ghanaian Canadian poet Dannabang Kuwabong discovers links with his Dagaaba people as he travels across the Caribbean.[7]

I would maintain that there is also something special in the relationship between people of Indian ancestry and India. This was made evident in the query "Are you from India?" that we African Asians frequently met in the 1970s as students in the United States. There was always that furtive glance even if no word was exchanged, when someone looking Indian was detected—even if they were across the street. This need to connect may have to do with the nature of being Indian; it may have to do with the nature of the absence from India, for example of being a minority wherever the immigrants have found themselves. It is something that might perhaps change in our times of mass migrations.

During my childhood, India was a place of the imagination—a distant place of origin with which I could not quite connect. It had been evoked for me in the edifying tales of mystics and devotees that I heard in our prayer house; in a few scattered incidents from her childhood related by my maternal grandmother; in the few Hindi films I saw, which showed voluptuous women dancing in fields on the one hand and grim social reality on the other. Relatives had gone there and brought back exotic gifts and stories of abject poverty. My mother in a morbid mood sometimes would bring forth a tale about the violence of India. (A man enters a bus carrying a woman's amputated arm adorned with a string of gold bracelets.) One uncle, of an extraordinarily pious bent, had visited there and returned almost immediately—in the same ship, apparently—unable to witness the poverty on the streets of Bombay. Perhaps such stories were meant to make us feel good about the place that was our home. But still, to my mother, India was also the font of our values and morality. The film *Mother India*, about the tragedy and triumph of a widowed woman (like herself) in a newly independent India, epitomized those values. Films were a luxury; still, she had all of us kids go and see this one.

Newspapers and magazines frequently informed us that India was starving and backward. We read about its floods, famines, and violence. About a prime minister who drank urine.

THE URGE TO GET AWAY

Our teachers who came from India we thought laughable: their English sounded comical and many of the teachers, with notable exceptions, were truly incompetent compared to their British counterparts. India, then, was embarrassing. We looked up to London, where the prestige lay. London was the home of Winston Churchill, Cliff Richard, the Rolling Stones, and the Beatles, Shakespeare, and Charles Dickens, Enid Blyton, and Agatha Christie and all the other books and comics we read, and of course the Queen and Prince Philip. It was considered a point of prestige to bear the hallmark "London-returned," i.e., to have been to London.

And so as a child I had no burning interest in my ancestral homeland. Only later, when I went away to the United States, when a sense of loss oppressed me and an understanding of my identity became vital to my well-being, did my serious and concerted interest in India begin. I read volumes of Indian literature and philosophy. I took courses in Sanskrit, discovered Nehru and Gandhi, who respectively charmed and moved me. I saw the starkly realist films of Satyajit Ray, learned to appreciate the music of Ravi Shankar, Ali Akbar Khan, Subbalakshmi, and others. Now India became approachable, a place to be proud of and to be claimed; yet it remained distant. For one thing, it was too big and complex. Where did I fit into its tumultuous complexity, its harried history?

A few people from my parents' generation had made the journey, landing by steamship at Bombay and proceeding thence. If they worked for the government, they were allowed "home leave"—a fully paid passage. My father, according to our family lore, had attempted the visit as an itinerant young bachelor, but was not allowed to disembark because he had no papers. Recently my generation can afford the trip more easily, and they can fly. Now that the embarrassment about India imparted by their colonial childhood is gone, and India in any case has become a go-to place the world over, many have gone. I had no burning desire to join these tourists, though I knew that in time I would. Just to see it, this India that was still in my imagination and my reading and listening. My opportunity came unexpectedly, after I had published my second novel, with an invitation to attend a conference.

I was full of trepidation before that visit—and not only due to the scores of health warnings and pieces of advice I was given. ("Always check your shoes for scorpions before putting them on.") I was going to the real India, on the ground, and unsure of what to expect and what my reaction would be to it. Would I embrace it or would I be disappointed? I did not want a "Taj Mahal" visit, a tour-book approach; I desired to see the real India, one to which I could connect. I saw an epic dimension to my visit, and felt that it should be done with that consciousness. Perhaps it was the novelist in me, bringing drama to something ordinary.

My impression, when I first set foot in India, in Delhi, was that it looked so wretchedly familiar. This was what I first observed in my travel journal. The long dull corridor from the airplane exit that could be anywhere, the airport hall with immigration counters, people jumping queues in what seemed a typical

THE URGE TO GET AWAY

Indian anarchy. The thought began, and it would recur repeatedly during the length of that four-week stay: Where *is* India? Where is that epiphany, that revelation that proclaimed: This is India! What exactly I would have happen was hard to say, but it seemed that the momentousness of that visit should somehow make itself obvious. It didn't.

Outside the terminal, at an hour well past midnight, from the small mass of people who were eagerly waiting to meet their guests, a smallish man stepped forward flashing a wide smile to greet me. He was Krishna Mohan, who would go on to become a lifelong friend, and whose smile would never seem to fade over the decades. He saw me off at the YWCA, a modest hostel with suitable amenities where mostly foreign visitors stayed. The next day, after waiting for some time in the lobby for Krishna Mohan, who was delayed, at the suggestion of the receptionist (who would soon be on her way, she said, to the Middle East) I took a short walk outside the facility to look at the medieval observatory called Jantar Mantar. And thus I put my first real step on the soil of India. The Jantar Mantar was a small complex of low, pink-coloured buildings inside a park. There was nothing spectacular about the site, which had been used the previous evening for some sort of reception; the ground was littered, and people hung about. No attempt had been made to glamourize or give significance to this memorial to historical Indian science. It was just there. As I walked around, I found myself somehow blending with the crowd, understanding to an extent what people were saying. I bought a newspaper. And then, on my way out, I heard a vendor swearing at a passerby in the vilest language. To my utter amazement, I understood it.

This rather banal, rather embarrassing episode acquired a significance. It told me, illustrated for me, that somehow, to some extent and in some fashion, I belonged here. I was in India, I was an Indian. The crude swearing became a welcome. This feeling was not contrived. It just happened. Someone swore at someone else, I recognized the language, threatening and obscene, recognized the drama, responded to it mentally with some revulsion. How could I write about it, then, as an outsider?

During that visit, starting from my second day, I travelled the length and breadth of India. Fortunately for me, but not for my hosts for whom I was a "VIP" and to be treated royally, there was an airline strike in progress and I had to do most of my travelling by train. Notwithstanding some trepidation, I saw much of India by rail, hugging the land, from north to east to southwest, back north and then west and back north again. A fast train from Delhi to Calcutta that I missed had an accident. I was fortunate in that I was in the hands of ordinary Indians—academics of modest means—who would casually put me on a motorbike (no helmet) or a rickshaw, or bribe a railway ticket-collector to find a seat for me, and away we would go. Everywhere I went, it was as though I had merely been away for a short time and had returned, and was not an alien. I made many friends. All the time I also remained keenly observant, alert to every nuance and pith in what I saw, seeking significance to everything. It was as though I were making up for lost time—the time my family had been away. And the epiphany I had sought did come, but in small doses. For instance, on my first train journey, from Delhi to Puri on the east coast, very early on the second morning I suddenly heard a beautiful voice singing. It sounded so pure and beautiful, it could only be a recording; but no, Krishna Mohan assured me, it's a young girl sitting with her parents, practising her singing; among Bengalis, singing is taken very seriously.

It turned out to be momentous visit after all and became finally a pilgrimage—a "Bharat-darshan" of the kind that Gandhi undertook on his return from South Africa when he travelled all across India by train.

It was immersion, it was connection, that experience of India, definitely not like the scholar-traveller Al-Biruni's, a thousand years ago ("They differ from us in everything . . .") or V. S. Naipaul's, forty years ago. For Naipaul, a Trinidadian Englishman, India had also been a land of the imagination, but for him it was "an area of darkness," which was the title of the book he published after that visit. As he wrote at the end of that year-long visit,

> like the Himalayan passes, it was closing up again, as fast as I withdrew from it, into a land of myth; it seemed to exist in just the timelessness which I had imagined as a child, into which, for all that I walked on Indian earth, I knew I could not penetrate.[8]

A satisfying and aesthetic closure, but it did not happen for me. My India did not disappear into myth, it had emerged from myth into a reality I had to contend with. It called me back, and

I returned to it many times, always to see more. The search was endless. Naipaul, of course, returned to India several times and later even married a Pakistani woman. It too claimed him, after all, to a degree.

The East African and Caribbean Indian experiences have been very different. Indians—mainly from the northern states of Bihar and Uttar Pradesh—went to the Caribbean principally as individual indentured labourers, and in place of family relationships or belonging to distinct Indian communities they formed comradeships of what they called *jahaji-bhai* or "ship brothers." Many Indo-Caribbeans became Christians, presumably for better opportunities, and this is often reflected in their first names. In contrast, the Gujarati Indians ("Asians") of East Africa came from communities with branches in Africa, within which they married and practised their faiths, and within which their languages, dialects, and traditions survived and evolved under the influence of Africa and Britain. They built their schools, hospitals, and community centres. The relative proximity of India helped preserve communal identities, and initially men would return to bring back wives. (The Punjabi Indians of Kenya, however, as I have mentioned before, in a note to a previous chapter, present a different case.) Therefore, unlike Naipaul, when I arrived in India I was hit by a rush of familiarity and recognition and shown warm friendship. During my subsequent visits, when I dropped in on my ancestral villages I was welcomed as a familiar by the local Khoja communities—all I had to ask was "Where is the mukhi's (headman's) house?" Moreover, I was amazed at how similarly we spoke Gujarati. They knew about Zanzibar and Dar es Salaam, and in one village I was taken to meet a very old, wrinkled woman (of supposedly a hundred years) lying on her deathbed who in a faint voice greeted me with the Swahili "Jambo." Hello.

But this is not to say that everything in India was familiar and acceptable. There were some aspects of India that I found utterly unacceptable to my sensibilities, and at times horrifying. I could never accept the tendency in India to define a person entirely by faith—as a Muslim, a Hindu, a Christian, a Sikh— and the presumptions these definitions came with, regardless of whether one defined oneself as such; and regardless too of the varieties of ways in which Indians have worshipped over the ages, or the regional and linguistic affiliations of a person. I was horrified by the periodic incidences of "communal violence" that occurred (one such during my first visit), with their brutal displays of what I can only think of as sheer barbarity. There is no other word for such violence against especially the women and children of the "other." And I was disturbed by the almost placid acceptance of such violence among enlightened, liberal Indians, among them my new friends, as simply how things were. (When I read a list of such violence in a newspaper during my first visit, I was deeply traumatized; my heart sank. Was this the India that had just embraced me? The memory of that moment, in Calcutta, remains vivid.)

The Partition of India has had tragic consequences; it has brought about a climate of increasing mutual suspicion and hatred across the barbed wire. To visit the Wagah border in Punjab between India and Pakistan is to grieve. I believe that

Partition (as it is called) effectively shepherded the religious extremists of either stripe into narrower spaces—the space much narrower in the case of Pakistan—in which to brew their volatile bigotry and bare their fangs. It has entrenched hard-line Hindu and Muslim identities, when there was before more flexibility. But it is a fait accompli. Pakistan is now an officially Islamic state with strands of dangerous extremism as part of its fabric. It mistreats its Hindus and Christians. In India, on the other hand, I found it hard to ignore the increasingly obvious secondary and marginal status of the Muslims, who are lumped and stereotyped together, seen more often as an irritant to the national vision. There seems a growing acceptance by the "majority" that theirs is a Hindu nation, a view proclaimed vigorously by the right-wing Hindutva parties that have been on the rise in recent times and now form the national government.

In the two and a half decades since my first visit, India seemed to have become more materialistic, less spiritual. Was it ever spiritual? The middle classes became wealthier, which was good to observe. Where my Indian friends once travelled second-class by train, six to a cabin, they now flew (and collected points). Their children were now professionals seeking easier, unencumbered lives in Canada, the United States, Australia, and Africa. It has been disappointing to see the popular culture of American mimicry and consumerism having taken firm hold.

Nevertheless, my encounters with India had awoken within me a dormant Indian identity. Even the disappointments that I experienced over the years were felt within the bounds of this reawakened identity. My world had tumbled within itself. It had done so before, when I went to university in America fresh after school; it did so again.

How would I write about my travels in India? I always took copious notes, expecting at some point to sit down and produce an account. A book about a fascinating place. My ancestral land. But each time I started, I was stumped by doubts and questions. I could not detach myself from my observations, could not stand back and say, This is India, this is me. After all, who *was* I? Where did I belong, and where was my audience? Did I understand my subject? Instead of "India," I was seeing the place in all its confusing complexity; a complexity of which I was myself a product and an example. The more I dug, the more there was. Layers of history, tangles of narrative. I kept returning to India frequently, obsessed with the idea of discovering just a bit more, just enough to call it completion, and thus to be able to finish the book. I had become the compulsive gambler, waiting for that one outcome. But India was endless, in space and time, and everywhere I went, there was myself in the way.

During a period when an industry thrived in the West publishing "India books" in all their variety, I could not complete just one after so many visits, with so much to say. Independent India's fiftieth anniversary came and went, the publishing world experienced a jamboree; the sixtieth anniversary too came and went. Finally, almost with an agent's proverbial gun to my head, the revelation came, as simple as saying, But the emperor has no clothes! And this was that I must write not about India but about myself in India. A book essentially about myself and my relationship to India. A book about my rediscovery of it, the assumption being that it had already lain within me, dormant. And that is what I wrote.[9]

My India was then necessarily different from that of the travellers I had read. Al-Biruni, the Central Asian Muslim, had come as a scholar and scientist to a foreign, non-Islamic land that was intellectually challenging and totally alien; Ibn Battuta, the Moroccan Muslim, came to a somewhat familiar culture, in that the ruling dynasty in Delhi during his stay was Muslim. He was immediately employed as a judge by the sultan, and his observations are broad-minded but still those of a travelling Muslim. Numerous modern travellers have gone with a sufficiently detached eye to discover some theme or pattern to write about in the chaos that India often presents to any observer.

V. S. Naipaul, like me, came to the country of his grandparents. But he came to an India that was still poor, he spoke no Indian language, and he remained coldly detached. He was an Englishman, albeit from a colony (Trinidad). I arrived much later, brought up in independent Africa with what I regard as a soft identity, acknowledging its several parts, and in many ways I identified with the country and people I had come to.

11

So As Not to Die: The Need to Remember

1.

At some point in our lives, perhaps because the future that's loomed like an endless stretch of welcome ahead of us suddenly rolls back and shrinks, the past becomes important and may even come to consume us. We look behind us. This feeling was heightened during the worst days of the Covid pandemic in 2020–21, when mortality stared us in the face, and no one was safe from a terrible death. Families and friends became a precious asset to reconnect with and possess once more. People joined chat groups to stay in touch, exchanging stories, music, and photographs from their shared pasts; the homes of their births, which they had willed themselves to leave behind for a better future, appeared now large in the consciousness, to the extent that even today's news from "back there" also was of interest. All this to say that the past had never left them, and the honey trap of idyllic nostalgia notwithstanding, the realization dawned that their lives had not been for naught; however insignificant they had seemed in humanity's scheme of things, their history and roots needed embracing. This, at least, was the experience of many people I knew in Toronto, Canada.

When changes happen at a rapid pace, and sometimes instantly, when rampant travel and mass displacements have scattered families and entire communities across the oceans, their members thereby rendered lost and unsettled, then history, at least in the minor key of the personal, takes on a vital importance. People need a space of their own in which to belong, away from the bustle of their public personas. Family histories become of urgent concern, and the very technology that so frightens us by its invasiveness makes this possible. It becomes important suddenly to know the little details of our past lives—and share this information with grateful recipients. More and more people research and write up their histories, for themselves and their descendants; they make connections to stitch up their broken communities, now spread out—mainly through emigration—in small numbers in cities across the continents—Vancouver, London, Dar es Salaam, Melbourne and others—communities that might have otherwise lived or expired in obscurity in this dizzyingly complex modern world. Escaping extinction, their histories and data will now live forever in the electronic cloud, accessible to all who care.[1]

I come from circumstances—growing up in an Asian community among other such communities in colonial and early independent East Africa—during which our own history was not deemed important. As a people we did not ask ourselves much about ourselves. Miracles and inspiration loomed large.

The future was an open expanse. Our high school curricula were for decades set by English universities and therefore we learned what England taught us. I remember learning about Lancashire and Cheshire as a young boy, when my elder siblings were learning about the Tudors and the Stuarts and cracking their heads to analyze Shakespeare and Dickens for exams set in Cambridge.[2] After independence, Africa and the world were introduced into the syllabi, recently packaged, but all "out there" and abstract. If this history was more relevant, it was taught to minds already honed by England. Besides, most of the brightest opted for science, looking to quick careers in the professions, and history was set aside, only for its absence to nag later on in life.

We were not sophisticated or educated enough; we did not possess written histories; instead, we had fragments of memories about India, and other oral narratives that were mythological and didactic in nature, relating miraculous communal and religious stories. Most of us—speaking of my generation, and as someone of Indian origin—did not know where exactly in India our grandparents came from, or when exactly and how they arrived in East Africa, even though that information lay right beneath the surface of our lives—we had only to seek out a grandparent willing to talk. We knew even less about the other people among whom we lived, African and Indian. Who exactly they were, what were their cultures, their beliefs. It has caused me profound regret to have discovered the ways of my former neighbours and townspeople much later in my life, when I'd gone away.

In my adolescence the anti-imperialist rhetoric of independent Africa had caught on with passion, under our charismatic president Julius Nyerere, offering a sense of belonging and an exciting and proud modern identity to a young person. Apartheid looked unshakeable in South Africa; there persisted uncompromising Portuguese rule in Mozambique and Angola; the whites in Rhodesia (now Zimbabwe) had declared unilateral independence from Britain and a racist government was in place. The leader of the Mozambique Liberation Front, FRELIMO, Eduardo Mondlane, was killed by letter bomb within a mile of my home. These were all African causes for which we protested in marches, the stridency of their slogans making them more attractive.

In the face of this burgeoning modern African identity our Indian-ness appeared to recede—though we ate rice and curry and daal, spoke two Indian languages (besides Swahili and English), and knew our roots to be somewhere in Gujarat. In Swahili we were called Wahindi, the Indians, those who were from Hind. Gujarati language was no longer taught in our schools; moreover, what we spoke and ate had evolved from their roots. In a reverse adaptation, among many Africans, a milder curry and rice had become a staple. Many of us preferred Hollywood to Bollywood, and while the romantic Hindi film songs were ubiquitous, it was American and British pop that drew us more (we even had our own Beatles-like band); our reading material outside of school came exclusively from England, and later also America. We had essentially left backward, poor India behind. So we thought; but it was always in us.

2.

That mixed identity, African, Indian, and British colonial, sustained by the exciting rhetoric of African liberation, an Indian devotional faith and its folk narratives and traditions, and a British colonial education and aspirations to go to London, was fragile in retrospect, but it had thrived in the closed and sheltered universe of a small Indian community in a small African city. The community was Khoja Ismaili from western Gujarat, the regions known as Kathiawad and Kutch. When I left its embrace in 1970 to study in the United States, I found myself adrift in an intensely challenging environment, grappling with the question, Who am I?—beyond the superficial description of my passport. I needed urgently to orient myself in this larger world into which I had just emerged, to feel rooted in a place and in a history as everyone else appeared to be; to be able to say, This is what I am.

Around me was this tumultuous, ever-churning realm that hitherto I had only read about in books and newspapers, preoccupied with critical global issues—the American war in Vietnam and the student riots, military juntas in South America and elsewhere, the oil shortage, the arms race, the space race, the Cuban missile crisis and the threat of nuclear war. The Western world was home to the great and influential political figures of the age; it was home to great thinkers constantly pushing the borders of science, literature, music, and philosophy. There seemed a comfort and confidence in those who were native to this Western country and civilization that I myself could not possess.

Moreover, in addition to the white or Euro American culture around me, there was the growing awareness of Black pride and protest, in literary figures like James Baldwin and Richard Wright, actors like Sidney Poitier, the *Shaft* films, Malcolm X and Martin Luther King, the Black Panthers, and the glorious popular songs of Motown and soul. But like an orphan, I had nothing to show for myself. Tanzania might as well have been Tasmania, indeed.

This anxiety was assisted in no small measure by the prevailing North American obsession with identity, evidenced in the bestselling book *Identity: Youth and Crisis* by Erik Erikson and the overwhelming re-examination of American culture and politics, with the simultaneous fascination with all branches of psychoanalysis and Eastern spiritualism, among my cohorts at the universities.

But my insecurity also came accompanied by the thrill of constant discovery and the privilege I felt as I listened to two of the founders of quantum mechanics, Werner Heisenberg and Paul Dirac. Was this I, the boy from Kariakoo, Dar es Salaam, who had been kicking its sand not long ago? To top this privilege was the sheer excitement of finally being able to afford to buy books, hear new ideas, listen to new music, see new cinema. To entertain questions I had never contemplated or dared before in my previous, sheltered life. And from there to the joy of reading history and searching for answers, finding out about the past, most importantly, my own—and thus placing myself somewhere.

3.

I needed to understand my origins, find myself. I said I was a Tanzanian, an African. I was born in East Africa, so were my mother and father, and at least one grandparent. I knew no other corner of the world as intimately. It was the home of my nostalgia, my longing. There was enough in the libraries about colonial African history and there were courses I could take to supplement the knowledge I had brought with me. It was when I had reasonably satisfied my hunger for East African history that my homegrown Indian-ness—the small rituals, the miracle stories, the devotional songs that we called ginans, and the spirituality—awoke in me. These traditions defined my other, non-African origins. But where and in what context in the Indian cultural universe did they belong? My communal identity had emerged from a fusion of Persian and Indian mystical traditions, yet who in the wide world had heard of this obscure sect? I realized that I had first to locate myself in historical and cultural India, where these two traditions had met and mingled, before I could begin to explain myself.

Here also, the cultural climate of the day came to my aid, or perhaps prompted me. Indian spirituality was in vogue, at least on the American campuses. India was not a material superpower but a spiritual one, exporting not software engineers or financial consultants but spiritual gurus of all stripes, bearing beatific smiles. There were large sections of bookstores devoted to Indian philosophies. I would finger those treatises—and despair. They were too formal, too abstract, and gave me a broad map of philosophical India. But mine was a folk tradition, geographically local and culturally specific. It would take me time to realize that a local, folk tradition had an independent legitimacy of its own, it need not bow to the distillation provided by the canonical.

However, connecting with Nehru and Gandhi had provided a historical link to India in real space-time. Both were from recent times, and they had gone abroad from their Indian homes as young men and struggled with themselves and their colonial legacies in ways I could understand.

Other students of my generation and mixed background who also felt the pressure to find themselves in history entered academia; for me the choice, after a longish spell in theoretical physics (which also concerns itself with discovering the unknown), was to examine memories, personal and communal, and historical data where it was available, and use them to tell stories. Produce fiction and a mythology where there had been none of the kind. Following the intellectual current of my surroundings, I turned—albeit gradually and not without the necessary aches—agnostic: there were too many questions and there was too much to know, and no certainty. The anxiety of being adrift had come accompanied by the thrill of discovering, the awareness that I could think for myself, and the confidence to do it, whatever the risks.

4.

It became a matter of pride and self-worth, of inner security, to be able to proclaim to the world: *This is what I am, I also exist!* Understand me, acknowledge where I come from, know it, it's a place as important to me as yours is to you. The new coordinates within which to define and explain myself were provided to me by history. It gave me a language and a system; through it I could connect to the rest of the world, to humanity. Religious faith, in particular my communal tradition, had shut me inside a cloud of obscurity, akin to a secret society, which few "others" could reach. Paradoxically, it had also gifted me with tolerance of differences, curiosity about the world, and scepticism about absolute certainty. To understand now who I was, I had to start somewhere in the past—hunt for a time zero, however illusory or approximate, and from there to move forward. Vain and wishful though this may sound, not to say naive and impractical, I had been sucked into this quest. I needed to find out, or at least to be constantly finding out, that point zero and the geometry within which it existed—the histories and the folklores and mythologies of India—in order to create a personal story that brought me to where I was now. And that constant search by someone who did not come from recorded history itself became part of my story.

Once, during an undergraduate course on imperialism and history, I sought an appointment with the professor to present her my gripe. We had just read Lenin on imperialism. I now had a complaint, born out of frustration: we studied histories of empires and governments ad infinitum, but what about the histories of ordinary people? Like my people. Were they not important? She smiled and said, of course those were important. There were some historians in Europe doing precisely that. I should find out more. Her thing was imperialism, the prime example of which was America's involvement in the world, specifically South America and Southeast Asia. She was denied tenure at my university and left for Berkeley. A few years later I discovered that in her answer to my complaint she had been referring to the Annales school of French historiography. A book had just been published by an Annales historian, Emmanuel Le Roy Ladurie, describing the lives and unorthodox beliefs of the simple folk of a fourteenth-century French village called Montaillou (also the book's title).[3] I could readily identify with the unorthodox and the obscure; but the villagers had been branded as heretics by the orthodoxy and cruelly rooted out.

5.

History in its usual sense, as an academic discipline, focuses on the larger phenomena, the larger populations, the larger movers and shakers. This is fine, of course, for we should know how the greater world functions. We all belong to it and are affected by it. We—the small people from small places—are played by it in some manner or other, and it provides the grosser coordinates of our existence. I might argue then that my presence in North America is not unrelated to the Cold War of the 1960s: in one of its policies to counter the attractions of socialism in the newly independent African and Asian countries—the "third world"—America at that time welcomed foreign students with open arms and generosity. (This policy changed over the years; the former open-eyed generosity was gone.)

The study of history comes from a long tradition, it has a language and methodology of its own, using (ideally) evidence, reason, and argument. It has its own history. It has its perspectives, its trends and biases. Moreover it needs to construct narrative to accompany the data, which may be meagre, and to evaluate past witnesses who may be conflicting or unreliable. This narrative is shaped by the historian's own milieu. As the Cambridge historian Mary Beard puts it, "Everybody has fictionalised history from the very beginning. That is what Tacitus did. That is what Herodotus did."[4] For long it was, for many of us, *Western* history. It was this Western history that we were taught as youngsters. It defined civilization and barbarism, rebellion, war, and terrorism, friend and enemy, hero and villain. It decided between important and trivial, mainstream and fringe, centre and periphery. And it hid from us its own darker motives as they pertained to us and its crimes against our portion of humanity.[5]

In Canada, and similarly in the United States and Europe, it is Western history in its many facets and modes that we frequently come across, in books, journals, and magazines. We read about medieval Europe, Classical Greece and Rome, the American Civil War; there is yet another book on Lincoln, Kennedy, or Churchill, another on a World (European) War. There is always more—and surely why not, the past needs to be re-examined and reinterpreted all the time. Not only is this history read and taught in schools and universities, it is also popularized and disseminated through film, television, and literature. The heroes of Western history become household names. It is now being re-examined in full force in the recognition of the ravages of colonialism and the genocides of Indigenous Peoples. But it is still the history of the West. However, for many of us, while we admire this tradition and even accept it intellectually as our own, and engage with it morally (we are citizens of here, after all), something is missing: what connects us to who and what we are, i.e. the recent histories of where we come from, and the ancient histories of where we come from. To the native-born European Canadian, we seem to have appeared like orphans at the door seeking succour—it doesn't matter from where, they've let us in. At best some exotic traits are discovered or acknowledged; at worst, we become statistics and liberal or conservative matters of concern, election issues.

Not only are the histories of the places we come from missing here in Canada, for example, they are also, ironically, often missing *there*, where we come from. Certainly, history is now written abundantly in some of the formerly colonized countries of the world. In India, the publishing industry is thriving and the academic wheels are spinning away as never before; the economy is ever growing and confidence knows no limits. Since independence much of India's history has been rewritten on its own terms. The Indian Mutiny of 1857 is often called the First Indian War of Independence. British imperialism is examined from different perspectives than before. Winston Churchill has been relegated to the status of a villain, responsible for the deaths of millions during the Bengal famine of 1943.

But India is vast; it is fractious; it still carries wounds from its past. It contains many peoples, many histories, many traditions. There, too, history is mainly writ in the large. The former Indian empires, the independence movement, the Partition, the various wars and skirmishes with Pakistan, and of course Gandhi are perennial subjects. But chances are that if you are away from the centres of power, the history of your people or region will remain in the dark—until someone wakes up somewhere and writes something about it as an example of the exotic or the extraordinary that India often throws up for titillation.[6]

Until recently the only comprehensive histories of Gujarat in English were those written in British times, the last one in the 1930s. In Gujarat, apparently true to the stereotype of its "money first" priorities, it is easier to find *Fortune* or a biography of Steve Jobs in a bookstore than a book of Gujarati history in English. (My search over the internet revealed only reprints and elementary school texts in Gujarati.) Recently while searching for a history of Kutch, a less developed region of Gujarat where my roots might partially lie (I cannot be sure), the only book I found was a slim volume published by a British administrator more than a hundred and fifty years ago.

In East Africa, and particularly Tanzania, the study of history seems to matter less. Monuments are neglected, historical buildings are casually destroyed, and the national museum in Dar es Salaam misinformed, at least as of the last time I visited. There are hardly any popular histories. The lives of the great leaders of the past have yet to be written in full,[7] though oral stories abound. Tanzania's war against Idi Amin's Uganda, costly in both financial and human terms, has barely been recorded; few people are aware that World War I had a theatre of operations in East Africa; and the facts of the bloody Zanzibar revolution of 1964 have been blithely rewritten by officialdom, some of its main characters erased from history. (Books long out of print give some recognizable details, and dozens of eyewitness accounts by exiles can be found on the internet.)

A staggering statistic from UNESCO gave the number of books published per year in Tanzania in the early 1990s to be less than two hundred; the corresponding number for the UK (in 2020) was more than a hundred thousand. One does not expect the 2020 number for Tanzania to have changed much. (No more recent statistics are available.)[8] Publishers cater largely to the school market, the few bookstores to the expatriate and tourist market (colonial-era books are still popular). A few years ago, when I was taken to visit a number of wealthy private high schools in Nairobi, I asked to have a look at the libraries. To my utter disappointment the majority of books were from the US and Britain, many of them hand-me-downs from departing expatriates. (When I revealed this observation to one school administrator, a man from England, he said this situation would change.) During the last few of those school visits, out of frustration I began my lecture by reading out a list of ten prominent African writers. The kids, very bright and chirpy with surely tomorrow's leaders among them, had heard of only one, Ngugi wa Thiong'o, who is of course a Kenyan. Once in a classroom in

Durban, South Africa I began my session with, "Do you know what they think in Europe and America when they hear of Africa? AIDS! Hunger!" This caught their attention. "Write," I told them. "Tell your stories." At the end of the session, a girl came up to me and said, "Sir, you will hear about me."

When you don't write about yourself, you remain unknown. And when you are unknown, you don't exist; or you exist as caricature. Not long ago the world formed pictures of Indigenous North Americans as bloodthirsty, screaming "Red Indians" from the caricatures of American Westerns. Lawrence Durrell in his *Alexandria Quartet* did not give us Muslim Egyptians but Europeans and Coptic Christians; Flaubert in nineteenth-century Egypt did not seem to have met ordinary Egyptians and had a knack for observing and mentioning women's "pudenda." The grossly racist caricatures propagated by Hollywood against Africans, Germans, Japanese, Russians, Chinese, Indians, and "Muslims" prey on the mind long after we've grown up and forgotten the movies themselves.[9] And a memorable sentence from Edward Gibbon in his classic account of Rome's decline and fall, referring to the emperor Philip: "He was an Arab by birth and consequently a robber by profession."[10]

6.

Many of us learned about other places through novels. They were our window to the greater world (Europe and America). You can catch glimpses of middle-class English manners of previous times by reading Jane Austen, you can learn about nineteenth-century London from Charles Dickens; about nineteenth-century Russia from Tolstoy and Chekhov. Shakespeare's histories are imagined dramatizations. Hilary Mantel, in her fiction trilogy about the life and career of the sixteenth-century English minister of state Thomas Cromwell, gives us a wonderfully detailed account of the England of the times and the court of Henry VIII. Obviously novels are not histories as such, they may not be factually accurate, they may mislead or lie, but at their best they do have ways of revealing truths and creating lasting impressions and empathy. They do expose another world; it's up to us to read between the lines or seek further. (Hilary Mantel's portrayal of Sir Thomas More in her trilogy has recently been disputed and widely discussed in the media.[11])

How familiar the kings and queens of England sound to the former colonial; and how unknown and removed from the mainstream of global events and culture are the places he comes from—their stories untold, ignored, assumed, or stereotyped. My first book, *The Gunny Sack*, set in Tanzania, was published in England by a publisher who knew the region; when I tried to get it published in Canada, I had to show Tanzania to the publisher on a world map. The book was published in Canada twenty-five years later. This is not just a publishing anecdote; it reveals how creativity can be stifled at birth by insensitivity and ignorance, how the stories of a people can meet a dead end and vanish.

Whenever I return to Africa—Tanzania or Kenya—I come to a place full of life—more so than Toronto, I often tell myself—thriving and bustling. People are not dropping dead around me with AIDS or hunger, I don't see children everywhere with distended stomachs and flies stuck to their gummy eyes. Of course there is hardship, as there is everywhere, and currently more of it in Africa; but besides poverty I also see kids with innocent, happy faces traipsing off to school early in the morning, loud wedding processions on the road, people debating Premier League soccer on a Monday-morning bus, vast open-air markets with an abundance of goods, someone humming a song. I see music videos on television, some of them imitatively American, others wonderfully original. I hear new idioms in the street, see newspapers and books for sale on sidewalks. Ordinary life that touches the heart and surely is the stuff of literature.

It then falls upon the creative writer to bear witness: to give his place a life, a humanity, a name and status in the world; tell its stories and myths and describe its rituals; tell its jokes, dissect nicknames, evoke forgotten streets, and recreate personalities; create out of its existence something universal. He remembers, for all.

When Gabriel Garcia Marquez had just revisited his homeland many years after becoming famous worldwide, he wrote poignantly about his urge to record: "Each thing, just by looking at it, aroused in me an irresistible longing to write so I would not die."[12] I interpret or extend this to mean that he felt the urge to write so his memory, his trace would not die; and by extension so that his place and his time would not vanish from the face of the earth.

A novelist brings his home into the known world of global readers. At the risk of sounding jingoistic, I would say he stakes a claim, plants his flag in the world's imagination. Uhuru Street, Dar es Salaam, or River Road, Nairobi may not be as widely known as Regent Street or Madison Avenue, but by God I'm going to bring them here.

12

Lawrence Durrell and I: The View Across the Street

By some unconscious feat of the imagination I came to think of Lawrence Durrell's life and mine as intersecting. Of course this could not be a meeting in real time and space—he was removed from me by many years, and came from a tradition and history as distant from mine as one can imagine. His circumstances were also vastly different. He came from the metropolis of an empire, its centre, I from its periphery from which as a child I looked to that centre with awe and envy; he was its sometime functionary and a luminary, I many years later its so-called subject. He was a writer from a place where all of the books that I read came from, I an avid reader who devoured anything that distant world sent my way. Our meeting could only be imaginary, and it happened when, at an impressionable period in my life, I discovered his most famous work. Here I intend to draw out from that imagined intersection a reflection on my own colonial childhood and my creative work that followed.

I discovered the *Alexandria Quartet*, and in particular its first volume *Justine*,[1] not because I was current with new world fiction, but through the less refined though ubiquitous reach of

Hollywood, whose steady stream of productions came to us in East Africa only a few months delayed. When I was a teenager, one evening, purely at a whim, I went and saw the film *Justine* that was playing in town, dragging along with me—to the best of my recollection—my best friend; it could have been my younger brother. I could not quite understand the story; its disturbing conclusion I could guess but not quite comprehend with my limiting and traditional moral worldview. The kind of sophistication required takes growing up in more ways than one. But the hauntingly beautiful Anouk Aimée, with long eyelashes and dark hair, who played Justine captivated a teenager in 1960s Dar es Salaam and thus captured me on behalf of the author. It was her alluring photo in the newspaper listing for the film that had drawn me to see it in the first place. Inevitably, then, when I could afford books of my own, which was when I began university in the United States, one of the first volumes that I purchased was *Justine*, in a cheap paperback edition. Only then did I discover the literary standing of the novel, the extravagant praises it had garnered in England and America. I ended up owning and reading all four books of the *Quartet*.

According to the author's note to the second volume, *Balthazar*, the structure of the *Quartet* was inspired by the unity of the three dimensions of space and one of time in the theory of special relativity; that in itself did not impress me, I was a student of physics and already wary of the trendy but loose invocations of scientific concepts in the humanities. (Evidently this has not stopped me from using a geometrical description of my encounter with Durrell.) What was impressive was its complex interweaving structure, its clever poetic language, and its rather unsettling ideas on love and sexuality that were sure to shake the foundations of any young man alone and away from a closed, colonial, and sectarian existence and newly arrived in the free-love, anti-establishment college climate of early-seventies America. The enigmatic Justine of dark despair, for whom love was love and sex merely an instrument, was enticing, as shocking and teasingly seductive to the novel's narrator as to its reader. This heartbreaking enchantress drifted about silently in a milieu populated by a variety of "foreign" Alexandrians—men grotesque in their appetites with features to match; weak women like leaven in the hands of predators; sophisticated men helpless in their loves. Love was the dominant theme and, for me, also vagrancy and homelessness. How could a young man such as I was, in the wilderness of an alien society, fail to identify, even in a small way, with the earnest, self-conscious schoolteacher Darley, a drifter now in exile on an island where he writes this narrative so assiduously in order to heal himself? The young reader might even discover in his own life a manipulative and self-absorbed Justine. The *Alexandria Quartet* was romantic and yearning, voluptuously poetic, intriguing, and very clever.

Through its multiple narratives and exotic, bizarre, and troubled characters the novels define "the City." The dark spirit of Durrell's Alexandria lies heavy on the pages of his creation, infusing the lives and shaping the destinies of his unhappy people. (It's hard to think of someone happy or contented in the four books.) "We are the children of our landscape," says

Darley, "it dictates behaviour and even thought . . ." Time and again he invokes the city. To explain Justine at one point he says, "as an Alexandrian, license was in a curious way a form of self-abnegation, a travesty of freedom." She in turn blames "the city" for their love affair, saying there was no such thing as choice. The city *is* the *Quartet*. It breathes inside the pages.

The idea of being possessed by a place, a thriving, throbbing city that defines you and lives on in memory, was intensely attractive; it seemed more and more true to my own circumstance, that of being away from home. Constantine Cavafy, the much-admired Greek "old poet" of Alexandria, looms large in these novels, physically dead for some years but living on as its mystical spirit. "You tell yourself," says this quintessential poet of Alexandria, as translated in *Justine* by that other poet of the City, Lawrence Durrell,

> I'll be gone
> To some other land, some other sea,
> To a city lovelier far than this . . .
>
> There's no new land, my friend, no
> New sea; for the city will follow you,
> In the same streets you'll wander endlessly . . .

How true these words to an exile. Or a foreign student who feels like one. (I must emphasize that these are the impressions, remembered many years later, of a homesick young student thousands of miles away from his small community and native country at a time when the means of long-distance communication were not as prolific and easy as today.) My City was Dar es Salaam on the Indian Ocean, a hop away from Zanzibar; more specifically it was the downtown Indian area behind the seafront, known as Gaam, with long Uhuru Street leading out from it, deeply impressed in my memory and sorely missed now that I had left it, having made a fervent promise to return. It did not possess as illustrious a history as Alexandria, of course, its provenance was less glorious, its mythology was meagre. But it was my city, it had formed me. Its geography was etched in my mind, in its streets in my imagination I could still wander about. To paraphrase Cavafy, it had followed me. It became my creative muse.

Dar es Salaam was its people and landmarks: the Ismaili Khoja prayer house with its chiming clock tower, blaring out medieval Indian ginans on a loudspeaker, the Sunni mosque periodically proclaiming the azaan, the horn dismissing workers at the harbour; the Hindu and Buddhist temples, the Catholic and Lutheran churches by the seashore, the Anglican church only a little further inland; the cobblers, tailors, and sidewalk vendors; the little grocery store on a side street where I would stop for a drink of water on my way home from school; the lecherous grocer on the main Uhuru Street; the crazy Goan known as "Two-elephants-lost" who would come shuffling by some Sundays throwing stones at the young men on the street who jeered at him; the friendly barber who came chasing little boys, to make them sit on chairs on the sidewalk and cut their hair. The imagination wants to say he knew exactly which boy from which shop was due for a haircut on his rounds that day; the reality is more uncertain. The beggars and lunatics and thieves who were almost friends, and victorious football teams standing in the open back of a truck with their trophy, serenaded on the street. Each corner of every street breathing with life. A city waiting to be written.

It did not have a resident poet (though poetry, in Swahili, was very much a part of the local culture, it was even recited on the radio and published in newspapers), but it did have its Europeans who lived apart.

In 1959 Evelyn Waugh passed through the city.[2] How easy if you were an Englishman, I have often thought: you embarked on a boat and sailed off on the waves. Brimful with confidence they could walk into any part of the world—teachers, administrators, businessmen, or simply travellers: the white characters of the *Quartet*, the white characters of Dar. Perhaps, as he sat on the patio of Cosy Café or New Africa with a mug of beer and a notebook, Mr. Waugh noticed one of my young uncles trotting along the street, having gone to pay his poll tax or renew his radio licence. And how did my uncle see Mr. Waugh with his mug of beer?

Justine had for me, then, a profound and even perverse immediacy. I seemed to be gazing at its European and English characters, and its people of the "foreign communities" (native Jews, Greeks, Italians, Armenians, and Syrians) from across the street, as it were, gawking, peeping at them in the manner of a curious teenager from a different, less-privileged society. They were strange, they were attractive, they were unapproachable.

The Alexandria of the *Quartet* is essentially a European, that is, non-Arab city. In reality it was of course multilayered and more nuanced, and Durrell acknowledges this, but more in passing. Durrell was in Alexandria during the war years 1942–1945, working as a press officer at the British Embassy, and the four novels of the *Quartet* are set in a small community of Europeanized Alexandrians caught together by a deep awareness of historical and cultural connectedness, though the differences among them are rendered significant; the locals are "Mediterranean" and therefore "Oriental." But the Arabs are only the background noise, at times viciously caricatured. We do not observe ordinary Arabs—a simple householder, bureaucrat, businessman, or even poet close up. One is reminded of Flaubert in Egypt a hundred years before, where he seemed to have observed (in his notes and letters) Europeans, locals in the tourist trade, weirdos, and prostitutes. Ian S. MacNiven, Durrell's biographer, observes in *Lawrence Durrell: A Biography* (1998), "In some of the more stylish shops, Arabic speakers and those wearing the robe-like galibeya would not be served...."; "When he in a temper called Egyptians 'apes in nightshirts,' he was repeating the soldiers' tag for anyone wearing the galibeya, and he was also reflecting the prejudices of his circle. Arabic-speaking Egyptians would be banished from Larry's *Quartet*..."[3]

Edward Said, in his 1999 memoir *Out of Place*,[4] describes a privileged class of wealthy Arabs in Cairo in the 1940s, a period overlapping with Durrell's stay in Egypt when he made the observations that would enter his books. Said came from a successful, Westernized business family. Even these privileged, educated Arabs did not belong in, and in fact were apprehensive of, that class to which the English belonged. "Schoolteachers were supposed to be English," Said writes. With Europeans, who lived not far away from his neighbourhood, "we had little or no contact." Once while crossing the grounds of an exclusive local club on his way home from school, he was told off angrily, "Just get out and do it quickly. Arabs aren't allowed here and you are an Arab." The boy had no chance to protest to the Englishman that his family were actually members of the club. "What troubles me now, fifty years later, is that . . . there seemed to be a fatalistic compact between my father and myself about our necessarily inferior status." Overall Edward Said has the most scathing memories of the English in Cairo, upon whom he looks back now with contempt. This is the other side.

In the same manner as I look at the "Europeans" of the *Alexandria Quartet* in wonder, I see myself gawking at the Europeans of Dar es Salaam. I am the boy across the street, noticed only as part of the native collective, who himself notices in particulars. In this way we connect: Dar and Alex.

The "Europeans" of Dar es Salaam and Nairobi were mostly British. The Kenyan settlers, in particular, have been known sometimes as the "white mischief" crowd and as such have been romanticized in British-made television programs shown on PBS's *Masterpiece Theatre* not long ago. Surely there is some significance to this selective embrace of colonial Kenya, though this is not the place to explore it. They were much more exclusive and arrogant in Nairobi, but even in modest Dar I recall a few "Europeans Only" signs. What was I in their world, a native—albeit Asian—boy? We held them in awe because they were so different, with their alien ways and superior-sounding, proper accents, haughty bearings and presumptions. They were from the same race as the exotic and enviable people we read about in our books. And they were wealthier, freer, and confident, leading leisurely lives, sitting in cafés, shopping in the expensive shops, dancing at the New Stanley, the New Africa, and the Yacht Club. I recall walking through the green and shady European neighbourhoods with their distinguished-looking bungalows lurking behind spacious yards; a nanny might be sitting idly outside, a dog might be running around. I recall being chased off the gymkhana golf course (somewhat in the manner of Said) by an angry Englishman, being offered a job as a ball boy at a tennis game, being taught like an idiot how to cross the road . . . though perhaps on that occasion I needed the lesson. On the Queen's birthday, I with my brother and cousins would go walking all the way to Government House to watch the celebratory parade, during which the governor of Tanganyika Territory—as the country was known—would inspect a guard of honour. Then would follow a march-past, and my heart would race with excitement. From outside the hedge we would follow the troops as they marched, black askaris, white officers. Did the governor, wearing a ceremonial black suit and feathered helmet, have a personal life? He most certainly did, as Mountolive of the *Quartet* did, though he was like a god to us when we were little.

And their women were wonderfully attractive and rumoured by the youths to be sexually free. "He wants to move in social circles in Alexandria and meet a lot of *white* women!" says Clea to Darley, in the third novel, *Clea*, speaking about a native. White was sexually attractive, as E. M. Forster's Mr. McBryde testifies at Dr. Aziz's trial in *A Passage to India*—"The darker races are physically attracted by the fairer, but not vice versa."[5] We used to understand this phenomenon as white-envy, but now we know it better as the sexual attraction of the unusual and strange: a different position, so to speak, a page from the Kama Sutra. They were forbidding and privileged, this ruling class that I observed from across the street. That is *my* relativity: not the three dimensions of space and one of time that Durrell uses analogously to structure his *Quartet*—those are too easy—but of people across a divide observing each other, feasting on each other, imagining each other.

Old Mr. Maundrill, a pipe-smoking scruffy-looking Briton, was our expert on Shakespeare. It was believed that you could not pass your O levels in English Literature without his assistance. He gave tuitions to the Eleventh Standard boys and girls, and a few times he came to our second-storey apartment on Uhuru Street to give lessons on *Macbeth* to one of my sisters and her classmates. (I would love to be able to eavesdrop, back into time: would relativity help?) Before he arrived, our cluttered home was frantically tidied up. The younger ones among us were consigned to the bedroom, to be quiet and go to sleep during this august presence, but of course we would peep out from the darkness into the dining room where he sat around the table with the girls, explicating Shakespeare in his drawling voice. At about 10 p.m. he would leave, driving away in his battered old red Volkswagen Beetle. A lonely old man, who was rumoured to be gay. He could have been a character in Durrell or Greene; I always imagined him so. He became a character in one of my novels, a gay poet understood neither by his own people nor by the natives.

My response to the *Alexandria Quartet* now is very much qualified by age and experience. It seems now somewhat overwrought and its characters stretched to extremes, the product of a feverish poetic imagination given free rein to create the most exotic within a closed Oriental (or Mediterranean) framework of a city that it also circumscribes and defines. The self-absorption of the protagonists is discomforting, and returning to it I cannot help asking: don't these people show any empathy towards others? Don't they notice anyone besides themselves and those of their own small crowd? There is a tendency in the *Quartet* also to typify—the Oriental, the European, the French, the Arab, the English, presenting rather disconcerting—dare one say easy?—national generalizations.

The conceit of the City as a world and a muse and its literary recreation, however, I do find in my own work. Could it have been otherwise? Would I have arrived here of my own accord? It's possible, I would even say probable. The City—Dar—was paramount for me anyway, especially after I had left it. It is not unusual for writers to recreate in their work a town, city, or district, or a street or an alley where they grew up. In this regard one thinks of V. S. Naipaul, Ngugi wa Thiong'o, Sherwood Anderson, Thomas Hardy, Naguib Mahfouz and a host of lesser-known writers. My question does not have an answer, and surely it doesn't matter. But I would go on to read Constanine Cavafy's poems, and I used Durrell's translation of "The City" as the epigraph of my novel titled *No New Land* (1991). It describes the lives and experiences of Asian African immigrants in Toronto who, though immediately upon arrival styled themselves vocally as Canadians having left Africa, and good riddance, lived in apartment buildings very much in the manner in which they had lived in the neighbourhoods of Dar es Salaam. The City had not left them.

For many years my City lay in my imagination like an open wound, raw and throbbing, until I was able to reinvent it and thus heal the wound.

The *Alexandria Quartet* creates a world of Europeans in Egypt. My world of Dar es Salaam was Asian African, and it couldn't be more different; I was secure in a religious community and a city, could not imagine living or belonging anywhere else. *They*—the "Europeans"—were the foreigners. I was, in a manner of speaking, one of the Arabs—the fixture, or scenery. But ultimately the unthinkable happened; I left my stable world of moral and intellectual certainties to join a world of restless exiles first in Boston, New York, and Philadelphia, and finally Toronto. Over the years my attachment to the city that shaped me, Dar es Salaam, has remained, despite the changes in cityscape and demography and my belonging more and more elsewhere;

when the political climate in Tanzania relaxed, I began to visit it more frequently. In my own way, then, I still belonged to Dar. Belonging is not a privilege given to you, it is not a choice you make; it is a feeling inside you.

Dar es Salaam then was my inspiration and it goaded me to write. The problem that I faced in attempting to fulfill this urge was, how does one write about a city that's not been creatively reimagined—like London or Paris or New York; how does one detach oneself in order to observe? How to *name* it for the first time, for the world of books and literature—which had nourished me intellectually and aroused my curiosities first as a young boy at the Aga Khan Library on Mosque Street and later as a teenager at the truly wonderful and generous Tanganyika Library Service on Bibi Titi Road?

What, how, do you write then? How do you write the City? You sit down and try to recreate it brick by brick, breath by breath; you infuse meaning into the past. You know you can never recreate the City entirely, understand it completely or at all; and so you create a form that is itself a metaphor for the city, or for the process of remembering.

The images I had when sitting down to write in Toronto were predominantly two: one a dark space, in which the author, a nervous and apprehensive god, turns on the lights one by one to give life to his city; each light a scene, an episode in a home, the location of a short story. Thus a street, a city, comes to life. Incomplete and somewhat discrete, artificial and formalized, but a recollection nevertheless. My first completed work was a collection of stories called *Uhuru Street* (1991). That street of my childhood runs through most of my early fiction—a street beginning in the interior, heading for the ocean and the world, a metaphor for the aspirations of its clamouring children.

The second image is a romantic one of a young man sitting down, having laid down his burden, a gunny sack full of memories, which he takes out and examines one by one. In the novel I was writing, I used the device of an actual gunny sack containing physical objects or mementoes: photos, a bloodied shirt from a long-ago murder, letters—each an impulse to a memory. Memories are linked to each other and to objects; in this way an attempt is made to comprehend collective memory, history, reality. The order in which you examine memories is to an extent arbitrary, therefore your narrative, your meanings are unstable. There is no certainty but the act of writing and the satisfaction of remembering, interpreting, defying the treachery of time. The result was *The Gunny Sack* (1989).[6]

I was aware, as a child and later, that I was growing up reading about a world different from mine, that of England and Europe (and later, America); it was an attractive and fascinating world, it influenced us profoundly, in our thinking and aspirations, even in our stereotypes. In many ways it beckoned to us—we wanted to go there, be like those other kids who adventured in moors and castles . . . we wanted to dress like them and speak like them . . . and yet not completely. We were conflicted. That world was brought to us by its representatives, the colonial administrators and the teachers. But I also distinctly remember thinking wistfully, as I grew older, "Where are *my* stories, when will I read about Dar es Salaam?" Now, with this collection of stories and this novel, I had written about my city, my people, myself. I had observed myself for myself and for an audience, and therefore I existed.

The Gunny Sack was ostensibly about memories—those of the narrator, the family, the community, and the nation. This oral history went back two generations, to our forebears who emigrated from India. But memory by itself is not enough to recreate the past; for actual historical detail, where memory failed or was nonexistent, I had to go to the written accounts of the colonial civil servants, the travellers, and the nineteenth-century explorers of East Africa. I had now left the romantic world of *Justine*; history, its reclamation for myself, obsessed me, as it has similarly obsessed many who come from broken empires, whose lives spewed out like so much debris during an explosion. In those first-hand written accounts I found eyewitness descriptions that were indispensable. It was thrilling for me to read nineteenth-century descriptions of teeming Zanzibar and its diverse multitudes, of the quiet harbour of Kilwa seen from the sea, of a slave caravan, of the Indian shops in the coastal towns, of the one Indian trader who had gone native in Tabora, who could have stepped out straight from the pages of Conrad. It was remarkable just as it was sobering and instructive to read the jaundiced impressions about my forebears in some of these accounts, leaving it to me to construct more credible and acceptable alternatives.

How wonderful it would be, I told myself, having completed that novel, to write about one of those mysterious diarists, a lonely colonial administrator; to approach history and the past not from memory, but from the opposite end, the written word, a diary. How novel, to imagine an Englishman writing about, observing, imagining me, in a manner of speaking. The novel that resulted from these thoughts was *The Book of Secrets* (1994).

You observe the exile in your midst, then you go away to become an exile yourself and later, completing a circle, you write about those others who left a deep impression on you—those lonely folk—the governor, the administrator, the teacher. Imagine a boy from the streets of Alexandria, perhaps from a street in which Justine goes to search for her daughter, growing up and writing about Darley, Durrell, Pursewarden. Edward Said writes about his teachers in *Out of Place*. There may be a curious coincidence afoot here: one of the teachers he describes is called Maundrell. Was he the same man as our local expert on Shakespeare, Mr. Maundrill, in Dar es Salaam? Said describes Maundrell as "bedraggled," which would certainly fit our Maundrill. They would have been of similar age. I have not done the research to check if our Maundrill had previously been in Cairo, and it doesn't really matter, but if he had, from Cairo to Dar es Salaam must have been a come-down; or perhaps a less volatile, simpler environment suited him better.

He was certainly respected more in Dar es Salaam, where he died.[7] The news of his death was given to me by my chemistry teacher, a new breed of Englishman, no less eccentric, who had come to us from Turkey. I was older, and Englishmen did not seem as forbidding as before; still, a few times when Mr. Edge would stop his car to give me a ride as I made my way in the hot sun to the American library, I would tell him, No, thank you, with embarrassment. I did not know how to relate to him except as a teacher from England. Finally, however, one day I accepted his offer and got into his jalopy, and he asked me then what book I was returning (it was on the solar system), then told me Mr. Maundrill had died, the service would be at the Anglican church. Mr. Maundrill had long since retired, their tenures did not overlap; still, as Englishmen I suppose they had a bond.

I would like to conclude by observing how time seems to collapse as epochs apparently fit into a lifetime: we've seen off the eras of the Cold War, the Vietnam War, Apartheid, and African and Asian independence, and we are living through another historical epoch, 9/11 and the Iraq wars, and the rise of China. What seemed unimaginable often becomes commonplace.

It is startling to realize how distant these people, whom I have called the *others*, the icing on the cake, were and yet in some absolute way so close; now they could be my neighbours living in conditions not dissimilar to mine. And who could have imagined that the boy who thrilled at the sight of the Mountolive-like figure in helmet with frills inspecting the guard of honour would one day accompany the Queen's Canadian representative as a cultural delegate to his ancestral homeland? That happened a few years ago, when I with a few others was asked to accompany the Governor General of Canada on a state visit to India. It was not for the privilege and excitement of being in a motorcade—I was always at the tail end, in any case—that I went, but to be up close to the kind of pageantry I had observed over the hedge of Government House with such awe as a child. Much to my disappointment I found the officials ordinary and bureaucratic and without a shred of romance. Times have changed. Canada is a modest country, and our ancestral India, which seemed so poor and backward to us in colonial Tanganyika, is a larger one and much sought after and increasingly powerful.

13

Whose War? A Blasphemous Suggestion

Some years ago I walked into my son's elementary school in North Toronto and, because his class was empty, proceeded to the gym/assembly hall. An anxious parent, this was what I often found myself doing. As I arrived, preparations were underway for Remembrance Day, November 11, to commemorate the end of the First World War. Banners were being put up on the stage, some with the Jewish Star of David and the Christian cross on them. I was astonished. I lived in a liberal, enlightened neighbourhood, I believed, and I knew enough about Canada to be aware that it was a secular country, and our school was a public school. I went home and wrote the school principal a letter, whose gist was, How do our children feel when they are not represented or recognized by the school the way other kids are? If you have to have symbols, at least make sure you have representative ones. Find out about the children's backgrounds. I did not receive a reply or an acknowledgement, but I am certain the message went through. It had to.

I have a certain blasphemous recommendation regarding Remembrance Day, but first let me relate an incident from memory.

In our elementary (primary) schools in Dar es Salaam we had something mysterious called Poppy Day. A couple of old ladies would arrive and with smiles on their faces visit all the classrooms to sell poppies; those of us who could afford to, bought them. They were pretty red things with petals and a black button in the middle, but we didn't know what they meant. I suppose that the money that was collected went towards the upkeep of the British war graves in our city.

Prior to the First World War, Tanganyika was a German colony and Kenya a British one. The British were determined to take over Tanganyika in order to secure the Indian Ocean and began an invasion called the East Africa Campaign. In Dar es Salaam, hardly fifteen minutes' walk on the main road from where I lived during my high school years, there is a tidy cemetery with a gate, lying placidly in the sun. I passed this European cemetery every day on my way to the library or downtown, but it was of no interest to me or anyone else I knew. It belonged to a past that was as alien and distant as the Egypt of the pharaohs. Now I know that it contains the graves of many of the British soldiers who died in the Great War in its East Africa Campaign.[1] Years later, when I was in Toronto, I had learned enough about that war and the terrible toll it took on lives that whenever I passed some lonely-looking elderly woman on the street, I couldn't help a feeling of empathy and the thought: whom would she have lost during that war—a husband, a brother, a father?

During my research for one of my novels,[2] in which my setting was the drama of that war campaign in East Africa, I discovered in the town of Moshi, at the foot of Kilimanjaro and close to the Kenya-Tanganyika border, another well-tended British war cemetery. It lay in a quiet leafy street of the otherwise chaotic modern town. It also was of no local interest, the Asian taxi driver who had brought me there stood aside chatting with a friend, and the two watched me curiously as I took a tour of the graves. It was at this border near Moshi that General Smuts, having taken charge of the East Africa Campaign after previous British failures, broke into the German colony of Tanganyika in 1916. One could not help but reflect, walking by the rows of graves, reading the headstones, on the young men hardly out of their teens brought from England and elsewhere in the empire to this distant foreign place to die. How were they remembered back home, and by whom? The march of the soldiers towards the Indian Ocean coast is captured beautifully by the English writer Francis Brett Young in his memoir *Marching on Tanga*.[3]

African and Indian soldiers were buried where they died and are commemorated by a cenotaph. Ruins from that campaign, including gun emplacements and a bunker, can be found at another town, Taveta, on the Kenya side, not far away from Moshi; hardly anyone knows what these structures are. The East Africa Campaign is but a minor footnote in the story of the "Great War" (though it merits a full volume from the Imperial War Museum in London).

It is an intriguing thought: a European war that today is seen by many as sheer folly or hubris, in which Indian fought African, and African fought African. Another operation to take over Tanganyika from the Germans took place on the coast. A few naval ships packed with new Indian recruits of different castes and religious backgrounds—and therefore not a cohesive or effective force—attempted to land at the port of Tanga. So incompetent and careless was this attack that the Germans were waiting for the British ships to arrive, and the hapless Indian soldiers were slaughtered as they landed. There are no marked graves for them.

Canada too sent troops to fight that war for King and Empire. (It is hard to believe that they went to fight "for freedom," as popular belief would have it today, for what would an eighteen- or nineteen-year-old from Arnprior, Ontario, for example, understand of freedom when half the globe was colonized?) Much is made of the Canadian contribution, which was undoubtedly important and cost many lives, and Remembrance Day, commemorating the fallen soldiers of that war, is observed with solemn ceremonies across the country, including a prominent, televised one in Ottawa. Poppies are sold and worn starting weeks before.

It is a noble thing surely to commemorate the dead young men and women sent to a war in distant places, many never to return. But that day does not carry the same charge for the new Canadians who have arrived on these shores more recently and are not of European descent. It seems at most a dutiful and patriotic gesture, goaded on by the media and promoted in schools. Many immigrants don't wear the poppy. In my experience, poppy-sellers, wherever they are, tend to ignore you as not worth their trouble. You might even call the red poppy a "white" phenomenon.

In November 2019, hockey season in full swing, an outspoken TV commentator, Don Cherry, having driven through the immigrant-majority locality of Mississauga adjacent to Toronto earlier that day and seen few displays of the poppy, broke into a tirade in his broadcast against people not respecting the Remembrance. "You people," he ranted in his familiar fashion, pointing to the screen, ". . . you love our way of life, you love our milk and honey, at least you can pay a couple of bucks for a poppy or something like that. These guys paid for your way of life that you enjoy in Canada, these guys paid the biggest price."[4]

There was a public outcry—the offence was egregious and blatant, divisive and bordering on racism. It was also quite ignorant, as jingoism tends to be. Times had changed; he could have got away with it a few years before. Who is "we," after all? For one thing, there are many people of German descent in Canada; some ancestors might have fought for the other side. And so the longstanding fixture on the national hockey broadcasts, always amusing and generally liked, was summarily removed.

Among the objections raised to Don Cherry's comment was the point that many Indians and Africans had also fought in that war. The descendants of some of these men and women were now Canadians. Proofs of their contribution in the forms of citations, medals, and photos were displayed to the media. A few weeks after this incident, when I was in India on my way to Pakistan by road, I stayed with an old friend in Amritsar, which is at the border between the two countries, and related to him the Canadian incident. I brought forward the argument that many soldiers who fought in that war were Indians and Africans. To which came the immediate rejoinder, "But whose war?" Now here was something to think about. It was a European—tribal, if you will—war, and without British imperial presence in South Asia and Africa, men from there would not simply have gone to fight "for freedom." Many had in fact been kidnapped and taken to fight in that European war.[5] History is full of such conundrums and ironies.

Men and women everywhere have had to fight and struggle to defend their freedom. For many years now I've entertained this blasphemous thought: shouldn't we use this day to remember *all* those who have fought for their freedom, dignity, and survival *everywhere* on the globe, and not only those who fought in the Great Wars of Europe? The wars in East Asia, freedom fighters in Kenya and South Africa, the Partition of India, the massacres in Rwanda and Bosnia, are only a few of the global disturbances that have cost lives. If we celebrated all those who fought for freedom, Remembrance Day would be a universal day.

14

A New Dispensation? After George Floyd

At the time of my arrival in Toronto in 1980, the English Canadian literary scene had recently undergone its period of patriotic nationalism, promoting local writers, but it was still heavily influenced by Britain and the United States. Bookstores and libraries, book reviews, bestseller lists, and book chatter all reflected this reality in which people like me were clearly the outsiders. Bharati Mukherjee, the Indian writer who had attained some renown, had just left Canada for the United States, condemning, in an infamous article titled "An Invisible Woman," published in the March 1981 issue of *Saturday Night,* the resistance and racism she had faced practising her profession in this country. And so we relative newcomers, more optimistic and with less choice, set ourselves up to define our own literary space, to introduce ourselves to the literary establishment, and perhaps start a dialogue and mutual accommodation with this Canadian mainstream.

Within a year of that arrival, some of us had founded a literary magazine, *The Toronto South Asian Review* (*TSAR*). In explicit terms, according to its first editorial, its goal was "to publish literature that traces some parts of its heritage and inspiration to the countries of South Asia." There was an exclusivity to this name that I personally found uncomfortable. I had picked it, but it didn't mean much to me, "South Asia" being a compromise neutral term learned at a university department while searching for roots. All the three founders were in fact third-generation from East Africa—specifically, from the same year in the same boys' school in Dar es Salaam. The spouses, two of whom were from the sister girls' school, were fully in support, though perhaps not as obsessed.[1] However, Black consciousness was in full force in the United States, and it embraced Africa in a way that, we felt, could not include us. And so "South Asian" was picked, a copout. After a few issues the focus of the magazine was acknowledged to be non-Western, or the so-called third world, and therefore we agreed to change the name to *The Toronto Review of Contemporary Writing Abroad*. The description "Abroad" has been confusing, but all it meant was "at large."

Contributions arrived from grateful writers in every part of Canada and the US who had been searching for just such an outlet. Many of them were academics in English departments of colleges and universities, harbouring literary ambitions of their own while facing their own struggles for academic recognition. In their critical work, which was their métier, they now began to illuminate and promote the sort of writers we published, from Asia, Africa, and the Caribbean, contrasting their styles and themes to the English Canadian mainstream aesthetics that was firmly embedded in the Anglo-Euro-American traditions and fashions of the day. Arun Prabha Mukherjee has called this trend in fiction and poetry "oppositional aesthetics."[2]

The journal (as we sometimes also called it) was well-edited and perfect-bound, printed at the University of Toronto Press, and its quality pleasantly surprised the sceptics who had expected stapled pages of community news and shop ads of the sort that could be picked up at "ethnic" grocery stores. (With new technology and money, the quality of those publications has, however, changed remarkably.) Following a few issues of *TSAR*, a two-day meeting at the University of Toronto campus brought together many of our contributors—in addition to Ontario, they came from Prince Edward Island, New Brunswick, Quebec, Alberta, Manitoba, and British Columbia—and an interested local public, mostly young people like us with similar interests in literature. It was a lively, exuberant event with discussions, debates, and readings, where personal stories were exchanged by the participants and friendships forged; it became clear that weekend that Canadian literature would not remain the same as it had been. There was such excitement about new possibilities in poetry and fiction, and their analyses, such confidence and good feeling that I was emboldened to announce somewhere that "the mainstream won't even know what hit it." An arrogant statement by a young man at the sidelines of mainstream culture, with no hope of getting in; envious, perhaps; resentful. What I meant was that there were so many of us already here and arriving, producing wonderful new literature, that we could not be ignored for long. Time was on our side, to paraphrase the Rolling Stones. But in the interim we still had to contend with—and protest—our neglect by the establishments.

Some years later, when we believed that the country was progressing nicely towards inclusivity, to which we were making our optimistic contribution, on a New Year's Eve, the CBC, our national broadcaster, put on an after-news special showing how Canadians across the land, from the Atlantic to the Pacific, were celebrating that night. From a small town on the east coast, which could have been Corner Brook, to another one in the Prairies that could be Cardston, and to another on the west coast that could have been Nanaimo, with a few other cities thrown in, the nation got displayed in all its diversity—as seen through a tinted lens that filtered out all human colour. Amidst all the good-natured camaraderie of the program, not a single non-white face. I rarely send letters of protest, but in this case I was incensed enough to do so. I don't have a copy of what I wrote, it was by email and it was somewhat rude, but I remember telling the esteemed broadcasters that there were more people residing in Don Mills, Ontario, an Asian immigrant ghetto, than the province of Prince Edward Island and concluding bitterly with, "You don't represent us." There was no reply, of course. (My statement about the population of Don Mills was not strictly accurate, I soon realized, but if we include neighbouring areas like Thorncliffe Park, it comes close. It's certainly true of Mississauga, Burnaby, and Scarborough.)

More recently, I stopped my subscription to *The New York Review of Books*. I had discovered it while still a naive foreign graduate student in Philadelphia, thrilled that a magazine existed solely to discuss my passion—books and literature.

The *NYRB* carried provocative, knowledgeable, and often brilliant essays; it was sufficiently to the left and not verbose or shrill. I enjoyed it immensely. But it seemed more and more that I was reading only select academics from select American and British universities—a handful—and though I learned much about art and literature, politics, history, and psychology, there was hardly anything about the world I came from. It was like walking into an exclusive party, where the liquor is of excellent quality, so are the canapes and the elevated conversations, but you are among sophisticates who talk the talk with passion and know each other intimately, and when you make attempts to join in here and there you are simply ignored. You could be one of the servers. You realize you don't belong, and—blaming only yourself—you leave. I wrote a note to the *NYRB* pointing out that there was a bigger world out there, to which I belonged, and received no response. After some thirty-five years as a faithful subscriber, I stopped my subscription, writing my reason for doing so in a small note on the renewal form that I feel certain some intern tossed away. (To be fair, in more recent months the *Review* seems to have its eyes on a bigger world.)

In Canada, until recently, a glance at the names of board members of literary prizes, arts councils, and festivals might have led one to conclude that a cabal was in existence (at least there were rumours to that effect), influencing the literary fashions of the day—what was in and what was out, who deserved the Giller or the GG and who did not. Canada already had a few dozen poets and story-writers from Asia, Africa, and the Caribbean—a large number for a small country—expressing themselves in exciting new ways, but they went largely unnoticed. To be noticed was a fortunate accident, and not without objections from those who said we were not Canadian enough.

But time was on our side, as I've said. Now, years later, recalling my arrogant statement, how prescient it was, as we watch editors, festival programmers, arts councils, literary agents, publishers, literary prizes, broadcasters, news media, and advertisers—not to mention commercial enterprises such as banks—scrambling and tripping over themselves with anxiety to prove that they are not racists but on the side of "diversity." In this new era that has suddenly fallen upon us, the *NYRB* is into diversity and the CBC proudly exhibits young reporters and anchors who are not white.[3] This turnaround was demonstrated dramatically in the television broadcasts of the 2020 Olympic Games, in which the commercials depicted almost exclusively Black consumers. Suddenly too, and as amazingly, a young, hip-looking Punjabi couple were radio hosts in a popular mainstream music program, their gleeful oversized faces displayed prominently on bus stops. *The New York Times* makes it a point to emphasize when a person of distinction whom it has mentioned is "of colour" (in case the name didn't tell you). Its crossword clues nudge you subtly towards diversity.

What happened to induce such a cataclysmic change of attitude? To be sure, in Canada some changes had already begun to appear, which I would attribute to pressure from the changing demographics that could not be avoided. Over the years there had been constant protests and calls for inclusion.[4] But change had been slow, insignificant, or nonexistent. The literary culture rolled merrily along as before, with a nod here or a nod there towards inclusivity. Those at the gates were mainly white. (At a reception during one Giller Prize event, an Asian writer came hurrying towards me through a sea of white faces, saying, "Thank God to see you here!"[5]) Finally, the Canada Council for the Arts and other granting bodies began to set quotas for the representation of "disadvantaged" groups in the publishing programs they supported—which take up only a miniscule part of their budget, the rest going to opera, symphonies, and ballet. Still, for the small publishers and the non-white writers the changes were welcome. And then happened the avalanche of rapid changes.

What happened was a sacrifice, the horrifying killing of George Floyd in Minneapolis, which was broadcast round the world. His cry, "I can't breathe," became a rallying cry of the oppressed and the neglected the world over. At about the same time in Canada the discovery of Indigenous children's graves at the sites of former residential schools further brought past racial injustices to the foreground.

Changes happened. They happened so fast, so obviously, it became embarrassing. For those of us who had worked for decades in the sidelines clamouring to promote "minority" writers, this change of heart and mind is truly astonishing. Of course many previous killings of Black people had occurred before, there had been numerous protests—who can forget the brutal beating of Rodney King? Or the global lampooning of O. J. Simpson?—and the Black Lives Matter movement was in full force. But George Floyd provided the pivotal point, the

Damascus moment in Canadian liberal society. St. Paul opened his eyes and saw colour all around him for the first time.

One cannot help but wonder what this really means. How serious, how sincere is this change of attitude? Is it just crass opportunism? Clever marketing? Running for cover? It's easy to become cynical when suddenly, in a single year, arts organizations start desperately searching for board members "of colour"; publishers scramble to acquire—and even send out calls for—"writers of colour"; literary prizes are showered with colour, juries are sprayed with it, and in a flash a prestigious poetry prize goes for the first time to an Indigenous poet. It would seem that this poet and her like had, in a period of months, sprung up to become "visible" and reveal their genius. The cultural universe becomes colour-coded: poets and storytellers "of colour" receive special consideration—favours—to the disadvantage of the "off-colour" ones. Do artistic excellence and integrity matter, in all the bending-over-backwards? Was white guilt so profound that the arts establishment became ready to admit its sins, show remorse, and atone? Do we now expect apologies for past neglect and bias (which may have stifled potential careers at birth and shattered dreams of artistic achievement)?

Overkill there is, definitely; in some instances it is just as definitely patronizing—a white man's burden all over again, or, in more recent parlance, "white saviourism."[6] You may have been ignored or neglected because you are different, but I say that the quality of your achievement has no colour. It can be argued, in reply, that overcompensation, though undesirable, is the price paid for introducing writers and experiences of genuine talent from communities long ignored. And in the past, weren't white artists favoured over more accomplished and original "of-colour" artists?

Nevertheless, nobody who is any good likes to be patronized, to receive a pat on the back, to hear the sceptics say, But she got it only because she is Black. Or Indigenous. Or Asian. In other words, she is a Token.[7] Artists agonize long over their work, writers take years to finish a book. In my part-time work as editor, I have seen and promoted (sometimes desperately and without hope) numerous good, original writers of what I call non-Western traditions—Black, South and East Asian, Middle Eastern, and recently Indigenous (because they too come from colonized nations). None of these authors would want to be patronized. They need discerning, knowledgeable, and sensitive minds to evaluate their work, not guilty editors and jury members out to fulfill a quota or quell their conscience. And they need enlightened promotion that dispels historical public prejudice and ignorance and creates markets for their work. A grant may publish a book, but how many from the public will purchase it?

Just out of my teens, I was thrilled to emerge from the shelter of a small community in a small country into the greater world; I felt proud and fortunate to learn the best from this varied world, its arts, sciences, philosophies, and to contribute to it my vision, tell it about my part of the world. I was happy to compete with the best. I come from a tradition in which intellectual achievement is respected and has no colour. We all have brains. I did not consider myself handicapped in any significant way, except financially, for which like many others I was awarded a scholarship and work—even if that meant mopping floors initially. I was as good as anyone else, one among many of different backgrounds, from many places. Yet today in Canada there are many who would designate me a person of colour, disadvantaged, BIPOC—the last of which to me has the sound of a disease. (Are you a BIPOC? Do you have BIPOX?) These terms are offensive and lazy. Conceptually, they gather diverse groups of people, blurring their distinctions, and put them—mash them is perhaps more descriptive—under one or another of a class of labels, all signalling: VICTIM! (In Britain the corresponding umbrella label is being discouraged: "BAME is becoming redundant. Blacks and South Asians have their own identities."[8]) The umbrella term is convenient for some, white and non-white, but I don't see my world cleaved into two. Labels are necessary sometimes, but they should be contingent and descriptive, to draw attention to specific instances of discrimination, injustice, or something else; they should not be permanent, defining a new species of victimized human. They should not be applied indiscriminately for political reasons or gain. By no stretch of the imagination could my colonial experiences or racist-inflicted wounds compare with the experiences of Black or Indigenous people on this continent, or the Dalits (the so-called Untouchables) or Adivasis (Indigenous) of India, or the Rohingya of Myanmar. To think so would be presumptuous and opportunistic.

In an essay in the *New York Times Magazine* titled "The Myth of Asian American Identity," Jay Caspian Kang writes:

A NEW DISPENSATION?

Today, "Asian American" is mainly a demographic descriptor that satisfies almost nobody outside the same upwardly mobile professionals who enter mostly white middle-class spaces and need a term to describe themselves and everyone who looks like them. I know many people whose families emigrated from Asia. I know almost no one invested in the idea of an "Asian America." And yet, while most Asian Americans may not feel any fealty toward the identification, that's the box they check whenever they're asked to check a box. And if people who look like them are being attacked in the streets, they understand that the attackers almost certainly don't care about the differences between, say, a Vietnamese immigrant and a Chinese one.[9]

And the media doesn't either. But the Vietnamese and Chinese do know the differences. Kang goes on, "... the immigrants who came to the United States ... who now constitute an overwhelming majority of the 20 million Asian Americans, do not see the country in such binary terms. They—we—are many other things ..." He points out how different the politics are within these groups, how different the income levels.

South Asians in Canada are more likely to see themselves as Hindus, Muslims, Sikhs, or Christians; within these groups they have their subgroup communities to which they belong intimately and from which they draw support. (Unfortunately, they sometimes carry antipathies brought over from the homeland.) Cultural and religious events keep these subgroups constantly connected; when, during the Covid pandemic, in-person gatherings were not possible, a plethora of online events and connections sprang up. If anything, communal ties were strengthened that year.

There *is* racism in Canada, no reasonable person would deny that; cub reporters from various media affirm this fact regularly by going around like school monitors noting down instances. The staid and once conservative bastion *The Globe and Mail* publishes columns describing them. I recall my nervousness about coming to live in Toronto, where I had paid short visits before. People were spat upon, called names in the street, and were physically attacked. (Bharati Mukherjee wrote that "in Canada, I was frequently taken for a prostitute or shoplifter."[10]) One Asian man from Tanzania was thrown down on the subway tracks. A classmate of mine from school was chased down a street into a subway and only saved by two cops who happened to be in the vicinity. (The subway attendant ignored him.) I myself could reel off a dozen instances of micro and even nano aggression that I have experienced over the years. Some of those insults nag one throughout life; such is the bite of racist insult. In one case, which happened in my neighbourhood, the insult was so hurtful that I told myself later, I am glad there was not a gun in my glove compartment. Pure rhetoric, yes—the only weapon I have held in my hands was an unloaded rifle in the Tanzanian National Service—but surely indicative of the hurt.

I came to Canada very much conscious of its racism. But I have to admit, at the risk of being labelled a sell-out, that much has changed since then. Speaking of South Asians, they have produced in the last few decades a Lieutenant Governor of

Alberta, a popular mayor of Calgary, members of Parliament and senators, numerous medical professionals, and multimillionaires. A South Asian has been appointed to the Supreme Court of Canada, another became the federal Minister of Defence, and yet another became leader of the National Democratic Party. Indo-Canadians have business and other connections with India, and many hold the official status of "Overseas Citizen of India," which allows them certain rights in their country of origin. Where there were a handful of mediocre Indian restaurants in the Toronto area, surviving on a meagre subsistence of spices, there are now more than a hundred. But few, even the most successful person, will deny that racism exists; I've heard the most moderate people say (quietly), It's there without doubt, but it's submerged or implicit. Physical racist attacks do take place, directed often at obvious targets such as mosques and synagogues, or a woman in hijab or niqab. And the problem with racist insults—the "micros"—is that one is never sure one saw it right; you over-react or under-react. You may see it when it's not there and fail to see when it is. And it lingers in the mind.

The ideal of a truly multicultural nation, not in the clichéd sense where "multicultural" applies to non-whites—Chinese, Indian, Ethiopian, Caribbean, and other neighbourhoods and their foods—but in the sense that differences are embraced within a sense of oneness—a unity in racial and cultural plurality—is in my opinion one to aspire to. Most of us who are (relatively) new Canadians did not choose to come to this country thousands of miles from our birthplaces to live imprisoned within impregnable, mutually hostile cultural walls, throwing verbal missiles at each other while demanding handouts and apologies ad infinitum. Canada has a history of racism and colonialism, true. Its treatment of Indigenous people has been criminal. The discovery of mass graves on the sites of residential schools caused such disgust and disillusion about its goodness and "best"-ness that the celebration of Canada Day that year (2021) was considered by many to be in bad taste. Flags stayed at half-mast well past July 1 into November. But Canada is also the nation that in recent times welcomed refugees from Uganda, Vietnam, Somalia, Afghanistan, and Syria. Immigrants arrive from all over the world. Over the past few decades we have witnessed the country approaching that ideal where it acknowledges diversity—not loyalty to King and Empire—as its defining culture and identity. This progress is sometimes hard to see by some, who note only negative examples, but those of us who saw Canada in the early 1980s or before and have lived and travelled in the country and witnessed its evolution since then, could not possibly deny the changes for the better. One is vigilant—or sensitive—but also optimistic.

To look at the dynamic or changes after George Floyd in a positive, less cynical light, perhaps the new attitudes are a genuine declaration of independence—by all thinking, concerned Canadians—from a racist and blinkered past, from colonialism into a new nationhood that acknowledges past injustices and its current diversity of population as part of its fabric. A country that sees itself as distinct, modern, and independent and no longer is envious of, or aspires to mimic, European and American culture. There will always be racism, communalism,

A NEW DISPENSATION?

xenophobia, Islamophobia, anti-Semitism, and other forms of discrimination, practised by the few and condemned by the many. If I were to go to Kenya, I might face discrimination in select circles for being brown and "non-Indigenous."[11] If I went to India, I would be labelled a Muslim, whether I actually am or not, whether I wear a beard and skullcap or not. In Pakistan or Saudi Arabia I may not divulge my religious views for fear of a lethal fatwa. The last time I faced aggression was in New York; it happened twice during a single visit. Was it racism or ageism, Islamophobia or anti-Asianness—or just my face? I could not say. In one case, at the public library, I reacted; in the other case I didn't dare. This was America. They carry guns. In Canada today I would always react.

15

Cinderella on the Outside

Surrey, a smaller city just outside Vancouver, is well-known for its sizeable community of Sikh Punjabis, who have lived there for more than a century. In Punjab, and elsewhere in the world where Punjabis now reside, Surrey, we are told, is famous and sometimes referred to as *apna Surrey*, meaning, "our Surrey." Properly, its status is that of a self-governing municipality within Metro or Greater Vancouver. With Burnaby, another such municipality, it hosts a thriving Sikh Punjabi culture. But the City of Vancouver is the regional hub of finance and popular and mainstream art cultures. As such it boasts a thriving social and cultural life, an exciting mix of people, legendary restaurants, and places to visit. A busy port with frequent ferries to the nearby islands, it also hosts major league hockey and soccer teams. Tourists flock to it. Most people would concur that it is a great and beautiful city despite the rains. For the denizens of Vancouver, Surrey, not more than an hour away by road, may look distant and dead, unconnected; but it's very much there and casts a shadow, however dim that may appear.

According to the city's website,[1] 43 percent of Surrey's population consists of immigrants (the majority of them Punjabi, as should be obvious to any visitor), and 34 percent of its residents speak English as a second language. (Surrey is also home to 22 percent of Metro Vancouver's Indigenous population.) There are many connotations of "culture"; my focus here is the arts culture. In the world of the arts, Punjabi Surrey highlights in the loudest possible colours the gap between the mainstream and the other, the downtown and the satellite, that exists in most cities of the Western hemisphere.

A similar situation to Vancouver prevails in the Toronto area, with Brampton (52 percent South Asian)[2] and Mississauga (20 percent South Asian, 50 percent non-white)[3] being the subsidiary municipalities associated with new immigrants and non-white populations. Here, the arts mainstream resides in downtown Toronto—its manifestations are the symphony orchestra, the opera company, the major theatres, the main literary festivals, the public library, the museums and galleries, the major universities, and the arts councils. The world-renowned Toronto International Festival of Authors and the Toronto International Film Festival take place downtown. Cultural activities in the suburbs—classical dances, music concerts, community events—do thrive, often attended in the hundreds, but they are rarely part of the national cultural conversation and are hardly noticed outside. Correspondingly, the flagship downtown activities are only sparingly visited by the denizens of the suburbs. But the mainstream, because of its status—its long entrenchment, old wealth, and continuing affiliation and reference to a once-dominant Europe—comes with influence and power. It exerts a centrifugal pressure—from here current notions about art, what's excellent, what's original, what's trending, the "what's what" and "who's who" flow out. The mainstream has the voice and presence. The culture of a city is often thought of and scored in terms of its mainstream activities.

How do the margins—the peripheries, consisting largely of non-white Canadians—respond to their subsidiary status; what strategies emerge to circumvent it? Is the marginality real or perceived, or is it only relative?

During the Covid pandemic, with the widespread use of online platforms for work and cultural (including religious) events, the strength of the downtowns was said to have diminished. Bleak forecasts for the city centres were produced. But this was an overblown claim, or sour grapes by those who chose to move away. The central railway station, the symphony, opera, and theatres, the major hotels, the prestigious private schools and the universities, the hockey, baseball, and soccer teams all remained where they were. With the pandemic over (though some believe otherwise), buses and subways are full again, the downtown streets are crowded, and more and more people go out to work and play.

There are global parallels as well: New York, Los Angeles, London, and Paris on one hand and the peripheries on the other, consisting of the small, formerly colonized countries from which many of the immigrants have arrived.

Europe in the last few centuries has occupied a privileged, central position on the globe; more recently, America extrapolates forward the civilization of Europe. English is a privileged language, and to a lesser extent so is French. But many of us in Canada have origins not from these privileged nations that have influenced, and still influence, so much of the world, but from nations that were once colonized and dominated by them; these nations are less wealthy or poor, possess little power and influence in the larger world, and use English or French as necessary second languages. On the global scale, then, we see the typical dynamic of the mainstream versus the marginal. India and China recently wield more power and influence; but even there American influence in particular is huge. In India, "English medium" school education is coveted, and among the elite there exists a copycat imitation of America. (I can't forget a model Statue of Liberty at an outdoor mall in Ahmedabad.) American idiom proliferates, and recognition abroad is a strong measure of success.

Here in the West, the reality of daily life and politics on those global margins remains distant and largely unknown; their writers, unless they use a major "world" language, remain as unknown as distant planets; so do their histories, their arts, their traditions, and much else. But we are constantly informed about mishaps there—their diseases and wars, their human rights violations, which only serve to boost our sense of superiority. The greatest vocalist or a major dramatist from India, a renowned poet from Iran or Pakistan, a novelist from Kenya or the Philippines will gather little attention in the Toronto mainstream media—which might likely be discussing a performance of an opera, a ballet, a visit by a British author. Only in rare cases, to introduce a shot of the exotic, or when artists from the marginal countries win a Nobel Prize or are political dissenters, and therefore serve propaganda value, do we hear of them. But England is the spiritual home of the anglophone mainstream in Canada; and, of course, like the rest of the world, we can't get enough of America.

Many of us, however, live in both worlds, the Western and the global marginal, and this renders us doubly marginal—as new arrivals we are not mainstream in Canada, and we carry histories, memories and concerns, themes and aesthetics, languages and dialects from somewhere else that is globally marginal.

We can think of the cultural universe, globally as well as locally, as consisting of many circles, each with its centre. They may overlap, be contiguous, or be entirely separate. One person's suburb is another's universe. A country usually has historical roots deep enough and an identity strong enough to hold its own. Within a diverse, modern nation or city, however (Canada and Toronto are examples), with their many small circles, the situation is not so simple.

There stands that privileged glittering circle at the centre, the mainstream. It draws attention, it is exclusive and commands many resources. For long it has been representative. For the overlapping circles at the margins it is impossible not to be aware and envious of it. The mainstream is widely exposed, and good things do come out of there. It is a dance to aspire to. The money and prestige are big, the lights brighter, the glory great—strong temptation for Cinderella in the outskirts. On the outside, she feels inadequate and a failure. Even others in her suburbia judge her by her success or failure to be invited to the ball. In Canada, which was marginal to the US and UK for much of its history, for long a significant measure of success was acceptance in those centres. For Toronto, the margins are its immigrant settlements, wherever they are, and especially in large concentrations in places like Mississauga, Don Mills, Scarborough, and Brampton. Suburban attitudes, unfortunately, are often colonial, characterized by insecurity, envy, worship, emulation, and a craving to seek legitimation.

For the artist, these attitudes and sensibilities are a destructive diversion, corrosive of his creative genius. Foremost, an artist must seek the inspiration to express uniquely—find a voice, a territory of her own. Where does she find it but inside her own world, with its sounds and colours, its joys and tragedies, its histories and memories? A writer at the margins will articulate his space, name it, shape and extend it—it is uniquely his. We might argue, even, that this suburban space is more interesting. It is fresh and vital, where the soul is, a forest compared to a tended garden. (How fresh the West African Ali Farka Touré or Baaba Maal sound compared to the predictable pop of today.) It explores new territory, what has rarely if ever been described or named or seen or heard before, and will have added to the achievements of human culture when much of what's currently popular in the mainstream, because it is so repetitive, has disappeared into the substratum.

As the printing press once did, technology opens doors for the margins. Today, online platforms have rendered newspaper endorsements and reviews, which were so sought-after and accessible mainly to the larger, influential publishing houses and made such a difference to book sales and author prestige, less essential if not actually marginal. There is infinitely greater choice in opinion on the internet. Social media disseminate information about books and book events to a wider audience; platforms such as Zoom allow promotion events that bring select, knowledgeable audiences together from round the world. These events are instructive, they lead to collaborations and new knowledge. Smaller publishers can sell their books and promote them on their own websites. Media bestseller lists (which were always demographically biased) are no longer vital when online vendors such as Amazon tell you exactly how you are doing worldwide. It is not surprising then that the loudest voices raised against Amazon have been from the entrenched mainstream.

There are hazards, of course, to the use of these enticing, even revolutionary alternative possibilities. Self-publishing is more democratic and increasingly recognized. (In the past it was dismissed as "vanity.") But the content may not have received due scrutiny. Online reviews may be fraudulent or uninformed; mass approval does not equate to educated appraisal. Uninformed facts may propagate. And internet mob attacks may amount to censorship. The internet connects people across continents, which is good especially for helping displaced peoples to rebuild their broken communities, and artists to find sympathetic audiences, but it also entrenches difference and isolation.

Nevertheless, these new developments do provide alternatives. An artistic career no longer hinges on the whims of a few editors and the appearance of a handful of reviews in what used to be "key" media. The gates are not few and narrow any more. Our Cinderella has options. Where else but on a self-publishing platform would one bring out a book on the political history of Asians in Tanzania? The vanishing tattooing traditions of women from western Gujarat? Stories about the beleaguered Chinese community of Calcutta or the displaced Christians of Smyrna? The sociology of a fishing village in Ghana? These are the histories and records of neglected minorities that could easily have disappeared; now they are on permanent record for anyone, from any part of the world, to access. They just don't happen to be a part of the traditional Western-oriented mainstream, which jogs merrily away along its well-trodden path, eyes focused straight ahead.

Often unbeknownst to the downtowns, the suburbs support thriving independent arts scenes of their own—reading and writing groups, literary magazines, drama and music performances, art exhibitions. In the Vancouver area, the Punjabis for decades have run writing groups, published magazines, and produced plays with social themes of local relevance. It is through their efforts primarily that the century-old history of Punjabi immigration has been recorded, in poetry, drama, and fiction. The generous Dhahan Prize for Punjabi Literature, founded in Vancouver, is awarded to a writer from any part of the world. (With telling irony it unites Indian and Pakistani Punjabis in the diaspora: both the Devanagari-based Gurmukhi and Persian-based Shahmukhi scripts are accepted.) In Toronto, Urdu societies have been active for decades, sponsoring concerts, recitals, and translation projects; some giants of Urdu poetry, including Faiz Ahmad Faiz, Gopi Chand Narang, and Ali Sardar Jafri, were brought to the city in the 1980s and 90s. Also in Toronto, the Hindi Writers Guild holds regular meetings, circulates a newsletter, and puts on drama performances. And, as already mentioned before, Toronto is a major hub for Sri Lankan Tamil literature.

These activities cannot be dismissed as simply "ethnic"; the audiences, which are brought to the public often without support from government grants, can comfortably run into the hundreds, an enviable draw for any downtown grant-supported literary organizer scrounging to fill up seats. They also demonstrate how the local mainstream can become irrelevant to those who have created their own global online communities.

The world is large.

Endnotes

INTRODUCTION

1. Multiple identities is a commonplace enough concept, but belonging is different, it goes deeper into one's being. It's what gives you a thrill, what changes you inside, or awakens within when you go back.
2. Discussing this idea, I have been chided, how could I call a place a home, where there are so many homeless or unable to afford rent? But no home is perfect; it is a place, as I have said, to return to.

1 NOWHERE ANYWHERE

1. Baroness Orczy, *The Scarlet Pimpernel* (1905), various editions.
2. Joséphine Bacon, *Message Sticks (Tshissinuatshitakana)*, trans. Phyllis Aronoff (Toronto: TSAR, 2013).
3. For example, the Citizenship Amendment Act, passed in December 2019, provides citizenship to religious minorities from Pakistan, Bangladesh, and Afghanistan who entered the country by the end of December 2014. The Act excludes Muslims and used, for the first time, religion as a criterion for citizenship. https://en.wikipedia.org/wiki/Citizenship_(Amendment)_Act,_2019. https://www.cbc.ca/news/india-citizenship-law-protests-1.5397915.
4. Perperim Kapllani, *The Thin Line* (Toronto: Mawenzi House, 2018).
5. Nur Abdi, *The Somali Camel Boy* (Toronto: Mawenzi House, 2019).
6. Sheniz Janmohamed, *Reminders on the Path* (Toronto: Mawenzi House, 2021).
7. Bacon, ibid.
8. Joy Kogawa, *Obasan* (Toronto: Lester & Orpen Dennys, 1981).

9. "Military History Library," Valour Canada (website), https://valourcanada.ca/military-history-library/internment-of-german-canadians-in-wwi/.

10. See Sven Lindqvist, *Exterminate All the Brutes* (New York: The New Press, 2007) and https://en.wikipedia.org/wiki/Battle_of_Omdurman.

2 VOICES IN THE WILDERNESS: THE NOWHERE ARTIST

1. Uma Parameswaran, *Rootless But Green Are the Boulevard Trees* (Toronto: TSAR Publications, 1987; Mawenzi House, 2007) and *Trishanku* (TSAR, 1988).

2. "Youngo Verma—Kundalini: Union of the Divine" (exhibition notes), Art Gallery of Mississauga, 2016, https://www.rom.on.ca/sites/default/files/publication/pdf/youngoverma_web.pdf.

3. Lien Chao, "Under the Big Tree," in *Spiritual Pursuits and Other Stories* (Toronto: Mawenzi House, 2023).

4. Deepali Dewan, "P. Mansaram (1934–2020): A Canadian Artist in, and of, the World," *Canadian Art*, March 16, 2021, https://canadianart.ca/essays/p-mansaram/.

5. Devakanthan, *Prison of Dreams* (5 vols., 2 published [2021]). See https://www.mawenzihouse.com/product/his-sacred-army/.

6. Memorials have been set up to the incident and an official government apology was made. Poems and plays have been written, inspired by the incident, and films produced. *The Komagata Maru Incident*, by Sharon Pollock, was staged at Stratford, Ontario in 2017. *Continuous Journey*, a film by Ali Kazimi, also examines the incident. See https://scroll.in/reel/938657/films-about-komagata-maru-remind-us-of-the-brave-and-risky-journeys-of-refugees-the-world-over.

7. Sadhu Binning, "The Heart-breaking Incident," in *The Toronto South Asian Review*, Vol 4, No 1.

8. Surjeet Kalsey, "Siddhartha Does Penance Once Again," in *Speaking to the Winds* (London, Ontario: Third Eye, 1982).

9. See https://dhahanprize.com/.

10. Dannabang Kuwabong, *Voices from Kibuli Country* (Toronto: Mawenzi House, 2013).

11. Wole Soyinka, *You Must Set Forth at Dawn* (New York: Random House, 2006).
12. H. Nigel Thomas, private communication.
13. Rahul Varma, private communication.

3   THE CANADIAN IDENTITY, OR LACK THEREOF

1. Cathal Kelly, "The Olympic jean jacket perfectly captures our never-ending struggle with national identity," *Globe and Mail*, April 15, 2021.
2. Ronald Reagan, qtd. in H. Res 664, 108th Cong., June 9, 2004 (U.S. Government Publishing Office), https://www.govinfo.gov/content/pkg/BILLS-108hres664eh/html/BILLS-108hres664eh.htm.
3. See Matt Lundy, "Canada wants to welcome 500,000 immigrants a year by 2025. Can our country keep up?" *Globe and Mail*, November 26, 2022, https://www.theglobeandmail.com/business/article-canada-immigration-population-boom/.
4. There are of course gradations within the group I have called WASP; the term often refers to elite Protestants, not for example, those residing in the Appalachians. However, for many so-called ethnics, the distinction is often not so evident.
5. See, for example, the site KHOJAwiki.org, which collects personal, familial, and communal narratives from the Indo-Ismaili group the Khojas from all over the world.
6. Neil Bissoondath, *Selling Illusions: The Cult of Multiculturalism in Canada* (Toronto: Penguin, 1994, 2002).
7. The Ismaili community moved from prayer and social meetings under school basketball rings to permanent buildings of their own, including the Ismaili Centre and Museum in Toronto and the Ismaili Centre in Burnaby, BC, where many events were secular and open to the public. Intermarriages were soon on the increase, kids grew up and went to university, and gays and lesbians became accepted.
8. Bissoondath, *Selling Illusions* (2002 edition), 106.
9. Michael Valpy and Frank Graves, "The contradictions at the heart of Canada's modern multiculturalism," *Globe and Mail*, December 14, 2018, https://www.theglobeandmail.com/opinion/article-the-contradictions-at-the-heart-of-canadas-modern-multiculturalism/.

10. See for example, Edward Keenan, "When Stephen Harper Refers to 'Barbaric Culture' He Means Islam," *The Toronto Star*, October 5, 2015; and Haroon Siddiqui, "How Harper Systematically Mined Anti-Muslim Prejudices," *The Toronto Star*, April 10, 2016.

11. Susan Neylan, "Canada's Dark Side: Indigenous Peoples and Canada's 150th Celebration," *Origins: Current Events in Historical Perspective*, June 2018, https://origins.osu.edu/article/canada-s-dark-side-indigenous-peoples-and-canada-s-150th-celebration.

12. "Some Canada Day celebrations are going to be different this year. Here's why," CBC Kids News, July 1, 2022, https://www.cbc.ca/kidsnews/post/some-canada-day-celebrations-are-going-to-be-different-this-year.-heres-why/.

4 PATRIOTISM AND LOYALTY

1. The online registration form of the Canada Council for the Arts, for example, allows one to self-identify ethnically in fourteen different ways, in addition to nine in terms of sexual orientation, to make up a total of 126 different identities.

2. Seneca, *De Otio*, qtd. Martha C. Nussbaum, "Patriotism and Cosmopolitanism," in Martha C. Nussbaum, ed., *For Love of Country: Debating the Limits of Patriotism* (Boston: Beacon Press, 1996).

3. Nussbaum, ibid.

4. Charles Taylor, "Why Democracy Needs Patriotism," in Nussbaum, ed., *For Love of Country*.

5. Stephen Metcalf, "Richard Rorty's Philosophical Argument for National Pride," *The New Yorker*, January 10, 2017.

6. Robert Pinsky, "Eros Against Esperanto," in Nussbaum, ed., *For Love of Country*.

7. Uche Umezurike, "The estrangement and hardships of a life elsewhere": An Interview with James Yékú, *PRISM International*, August 5, 2021, https://prismmagazine.ca/2021/08/05/the-estrangement-and-hardships-of-a-life-elsewhere-an-interview-with-james-yeku/.

8. See "Hindus, the 'Tebbit Test' & Terrorism in London," *Hindu Perspective*, February 17, 2013, and https://en.wikipedia.org/wiki/Cricket_test.

9. See, for example, "The Rosenbergs were executed for spying in 1953: Can their sons reveal the truth?" https://www.theguardian.com/world/2021/

jun/19/rosenbergs-executed-for-spying-1953-can-sons-reveal-truth; also, Anne Sebba, *Ethel Rosenberg: A Cold War Tragedy* (New York: St. Martin's Press, 2021).

10. Barbara Bray, *In the Name of Identity: Violence and the Need to Belong*, trans. Amin Maalouf (New York: Arcade, 2012).

11. See, for example, Esra Ari, "How I Became an Alevi Muslim Woman" in *Migration and Identity Through Creative Writing*, ed. Alka Kumar and Anna Triandafyllidou (Open Access: Springer, 2024).

12. See, for example, Philip Roth, "I Have Fallen in Love with American Names," *The New Yorker*, June 5 & 12, 2017.

5 WRITING TO SOMEBODY, SOMEWHERE: THE TELLING IS NOT EASY

1. Arun Prabha Mukherjee of York University has produced a cogent critique of universalism in her book *Oppositional Aesthetics: Readings from a Hyphenated Space* (Toronto: TSAR, 1994), in which she contrasts the works of immigrant and mainstream Canadian writers.

2. Anthony Burgess, "Belli in English," *TLS: Times Literary Supplement*, Issue 5943, February 24, 2017.

3. Raja Rao, "Author's Foreword," *Kanthapura* (London: George Allen & Unwin Ltd., 1938; rpt. New Delhi: Penguin, 2014).

4. Ernesto Sabato, quoted in Adam Feinstein, "Writing a Homeland," *Times Literary Supplement*, April 22, 2005.

5. Wole Soyinka, *Poems of Black Africa* (New York: Farrar, Straus and Giroux, 1975).

6. W. G. Sebald, *Austerlitz*, trans. Anthea Bell (New York: Random House, 2001).

7. Some of them have been written in Canada by Asian immigrants. See Zul Premji, *Malaria Memoirs*; Mohamed Keshavjee, *Into that Heaven of Freedom: The impact of apartheid on an Indian family's diasporic history* (Mawenzi House, 2021 and 2016 respectively). The website KHOJAwiki.org collects family biographies of Ismailis with their origins in Kutch and Kathiyawad, Gujarat.

8. See Abdi Latif Dahir, "Turning Nairobi's Public Libraries Into 'Palaces for the People,'" *New York Times*, February 4, 2023, https://www.nytimes.com/2023/02/04/books/nairobi-kenya-books-library.html.

9. I have described these locals, Asians and Africans, in my travel memoir, *And Home Was Kariakoo* (2014). A colourful character among them was the trader Musa Mzuri (Good Musa), originally from Surat, Gujarat, who it turns out pointed John Speke towards Lake Victoria and a great river that flowed out from there. We call it the Nile. Speke has been attributed with discovering that source. A guide from the Yao tribe, called Bombay, was equally colourful.

10. The Wikipedia entry for John Hanning Speke says:
"Whilst staying at the court Speke was given two girls aged about 12 and 18 from the entourage of the Queen Mother. Speke appears to have had sexual relations with both of them, before handing over the youngest (whom he named 'Kahala') to another man. Speke fell in love with the elder girl, 'Meri,' according to his diaries (which were redacted when they were published as books later)." https://en.wikipedia.org/wiki/John_Hanning_Speke.

6 NOWHERE IN AFRICA

1. See Charles Miller, *The Lunatic Express* (New York: MacMillan, 1971). According to this source, a total of 31,983 Indian indentured labourers were brought from Punjab to Kenya.

2. Unfortunately, Indian scholars have often confused the Indian Gujarati immigrants, who arrived as independent traders in Zanzibar and on the coast in the nineteenth century and even before, with the Punjabi indentured labourers who were brought to Kenya later. More egregiously, this conflation has gone on to embrace indentured workers in South Africa and the Caribbean. It is also not often realized that Indian immigration to East Africa happened in waves. Many professionals—doctors, lawyers, and teachers—arrived in the mid-twentieth century, mainly to Kenya.

3. "Tanzania" appears in the second stanza of the anthem. So strong was the sense of African solidarity in those days that there were no qualms about putting "Africa" in the first line.

4. Bahadur Tejani, *Day After Tomorrow* (Nairobi: EALB, 1971).

5. The expulsion, from the Asian point of view, has been described in several creative works, some of which are the novels *In a Brown Mantle* (Peter Nazareth, Nairobi: EALB, 1972) and *Where the Air Is Sweet* (Tasneem Jamal, Toronto: Harper Collins, 2017) and the drama *Ninety Days* by Salim Rahemtulla (premiered 2022, PAL Studio Theatre, Vancouver).

7 AM I A CANADIAN WRITER?

1. Adrian De Leon, Téa Mutonji, and Natasha Ramoutar, eds., *Feel Ways* (Toronto: Mawenzi House, 2021).

2. Linda Zhang, ed., *Reimagining Chinatown* (Toronto: Mawenzi House, 2023).

8 NOWHERE WITH GOD: UNEASY CONFESSIONS OF A SYNCRETIST

1. The Asian African writer Bahadur Tejani (for more about him, see p.94) said in an interview, "My father would recite the Ramayana or the Mahabharata, Indian epics dating back to 500 B.C. and he would assign parts for us to enact dramatic scenes, often partaking in the action himself." Annie K. Koshi, "An Interview with Bahadur Tejani," *Ufahamu: A Journal of African Studies* 21, 3, 1993.

2. See, for example, the book *Gendered Islamophobia* by Monia Mazigh (Toronto: Mawenzi House, 2023), where such incidents are listed in some detail. A Google search for "mosque attack" lists, surprisingly, more results for Canada than one might blithely expect. The January 2017 mosque shooting in Quebec City was perhaps the most shocking such attack.

3. The Ismaili imams appeared in modern times as the embodiments of the tenth avatar prophesized by Pir Sadardin.

4. The theory has been put about that nuggets of Islam were embedded inside the ginans, to be discovered later, as though a plot had been hatched in some eastern medieval Pentagon to dupe (not the word used) simple Gujarati folk into becoming Muslims. These nuggets would be like the "moles" of modern spy novels, to be awakened later, or little time bombs.

    Another theory says that the Khojas hid their true Ismaili identities out of fear of their Hindu neighbours. But when the pirs went about in Gujarat, it was ruled by Muslim sultans; it was the Muslim orthodoxy they should have feared—as the Ismailis (called Baatins) did in Persia, as they sometimes fear in some Muslim countries even today.

5. "Democratic freedoms include not just the freedom to speak and dissent but the freedom to worship. In the 'new India' this is becoming difficult because gangs of thugs have started wandering about our cities seeking out helpless Muslims and ordering them to say 'Jai Shri Ram' or risk being beaten within an inch of their lives. Sometimes they are beaten up even as they say 'Jai Shri Ram' in voices trembling with fear." Tavleen Singh, "Time to Speak for Liberalism," *Indian Express*, September 26, 2021.

6. Perhaps there is some hope. Now and then a recited ginan gets sent out to a chat group. This is a tendency mainly among the older generation, those (I guess) mainly sixty and over; occasionally a girl of eight might recite a ginan in a beautiful voice—a grandmother, one presumes, has been at work. And during the Covid shutdown I heard a ginan on my partner's chat, in which Krishna and Arjun converse, as they do in the Gita. This was not only beautifully rendered, it was delightful in another way: I had never before heard a ginan in which Arjun appeared. As I have said in these pages, his older brother, the softer-hearted Yudhisthira, appears prominently in the ginans. This ginan, or the observation just made, would mean nothing to the younger crowd.

9 GANDHI: DISCOVERY AND REAPPRAISAL

1. Some details of Gandhi's life in this chapter are taken from Joseph Lelyveld, *Great Soul: Mahatma Gandhi and His Struggle With India* (New York: Knopf, 2011).

2. M. K. Gandhi, *An Autobiography* (Toronto: Fitzhenry and Whiteside, 2011). This chapter is an extended version of my introduction to this Canadian edition.

3. Jawaharlal Nehru, *Toward Freedom: The Autobiography of Jawaharlal Nehru* (Boston: Beacon Press, 1958).

4. Erik Erikson, *Gandhi's Truth* (New York: Norton, 1969).

5. See, for example, Lelyveld, 43-44.

6. Uma Majmudar, *Gandhi's Pilgrimage of Faith: From Darkness to Light* (Albany: SUNY, 2005).

7. https://timesofindia.indiatimes.com/where-krishna-meets-mohammed/articleshow/474894.cms. For more on the Pranamis, see Mehul Devkala, "Mahamati, Mahatma and the Syncretism of the Pranamis, an Unknown Chapter in the Life of Gandhi," *The Wire*, October 2, 2022, https://thewire.in/history/life-of-mahatma-gandhi-pranami-sect-mahamati.

8. My community, the Khojas, were also Vaishnavite Gujarati, and we worshipped Krishna and Ali interchangeably, as I have described in chapter 8. Interestingly, therefore, many Khojas have roots in the region where the Pranami sect was founded. Muhammadali Jinnah of Pakistan also had deep Gujarati roots. His family were Khojas from the town of Paneli, less than a hundred miles from Porbandar, Gandhi's (and my maternal grandfather's) birthplace. Jinnah's family name was Meghji

Punja or Meghani Punja. Due to his exalted status in Islamic Pakistan, this bit of information is not bandied about either.

9. "'Hinduism,' [Robert Eric] Frykenberg argues, is neither the unchanging age-old entity of *Hindutva* imagination nor the purely Western Orientalist invention of some modern historiography, but rather a construction jointly pieced together in the eighteenth and nineteenth centuries by both Indian and European scholars concerned in typical Enlightenment fashion to clarify, codify and systematize the bewildering variety of religious belief and practice which came to light as the expansion of British territorial control opened up new vistas of knowledge to Indians and Britons alike." Brian Stanley, reviewing *Christianity in India* by Robert Eric Frykenberg: "Thomas's tribe," *Times Literary Supplement* no. 5524, February 13, 2009.

10. https://navayana.org/blog/2014/09/30/but-can-we-sweep-caste-away/?v=35357b9c8fe4.

11. See, for one example, the life story *Joothan: An Untouchable's life*. Omprakash Valmiki, trans. Arun Prabha Mukherjee (New York: Columbia UP, 2008).

12. See, for example, "Manchester council urged to reject statue of 'anti-black racist' Gandhi," https://www.theguardian.com/world/2019/oct/17/manchester-council-urged-reject-mahatma-gandhi-statue-racism. See also, "Was Mahatma Gandhi a racist?" https://www.bbc.com/news/world-asia-india-34265882.

13. Lynn Burnett, "Gandhi's Connections with Booker T. Washington, W. E. B. Du Bois, and Marcus Garvey," CrossCulturalSolidarity.com, https://crossculturalsolidarity.com/gandhis-connections-with-booker-t-washington-w-e-b-du-bois-and-marcus-garvey/.

14. For Gandhi and the Black civil rights movement, see also Paul R. Dekar, "Gandhi's Influence on the Civil Rights Movement in the United States," October 2, 2020, https://forusa.org/gandhis-influence-on-the-civil-rights-movement-in-the-united-states/.

15. Burnett, "Gandhi's Connections with Booker T. Washington, W. E. B. Du Bois, and Marcus Garvey."

16. Mohandas K. Gandhi to President Franklin D. Roosevelt, July 1, 1942, https://history.state.gov/historicaldocuments/frus1942v01/d575.

17. Mohandas K. Gandhi to W. E. B. Du Bois, https://credo.library.umass.edu/view/full/mums312-b181-i614.

I am indebted to Dr. Alok Bhalla of Delhi for the information and references in this section regarding Gandhi and the Black civil rights movement.

10 THE URGE TO GET AWAY: FINDING INDIA

1. Ibn Battuta, *Travels in Asia and Africa 1325-1354*, translated and selected by H. A. R. Gibb (London: Routledge & Kegan Paul Ltd, 1929 [and in various reprint editions]).

2. Al-Biruni, *Alberuni's India*, trans. Edward Sachau (New York: Norton, 1971).

3. Xuanzang, *The Great Tang Dynasty Record of the Western Regions*, trans. Li Rongxi (Berkeley: BDK America, 2006). See also Shaman Hwui Li, *The Life of Hiuen Tsiang*, trans. Samuel Beal (New Delhi: Rupa, 2011).

4. See *The Monkey and the Monk* (abridged version of *Journey to the West*), trans. Anthony C. Yu (Chicago: University of Chicago Press, 2006).

5. Gustave Flaubert, *Flaubert in Egypt*, edited and translated by Francis Steegmuller (Chicago: Academy Chicago, 1979).

6. Those who come directly from India (and there are many these days) would find this impossibly romantic. How they miss the point.

7. Wole Soyinka, *You Must Set Forth at Dawn* (New York: Random House, 2007); Dannabang Kuwabong, *Sargasso Sea Scrolls* (Toronto: Mawenzi House, 2023).

8. V. S. Naipaul, *An Area of Darkness* (London: André Deutsch Ltd., 1964).

9. M.G. Vassanji, *A Place Within: Rediscovering India* (Toronto: Doubleday Canada, 2008).

11 SO AS NOT TO DIE: THE NEED TO REMEMBER

1. The online site KHOJAwiki.org collects personal and family histories of the Khoja (Indian) Ismailis, making connections across continents, thus reviving history and identity previously consigned to oblivion.

2. In Toronto I met a professor who had been a marker for the overseas exams. He claimed not to have been impressed by the standards—whether of the questions or the answers, I was not sure.

3. Emmanuel Le Roy Ladurie, *Montaillou: The Promised Land of Error*, trans. Barbara Bray (New York: Vintage, 1979).

4. Mary Beard, qtd. in "Missing pieces; The trouble with history," *The Economist*, June 12, 2021, https://www.economist.com/books-and-arts/2021/06/12/the-trouble-with-the-past.

5. The 1992 book *Exterminate All the Brutes*, by Sven Lindqvist, quotes

first-hand accounts of the most abominable cruelties inflicted by Europeans in the Congo in the early twentieth century. When we read about or see the chaos in Congo today, it is good to bear this in mind.

6. But in India history has not only been rewritten but also re-rewritten in a climate of Hindu nationalism. Any associations with Muslim sultans and emperors of the past are under attack. City and street names are being changed, textbooks altered. Gandhi's assassin, Nathuram Godse, is now lionized or worshipped by many, and Gandhi himself sometimes regarded with contempt.

7. However, recently (2020) an impressive three-volume biography of Julius Nyerere has appeared: *Development as Rebellion: A Biography of Julius Nyerere* by Saida Yahya-Othman, Ng'wanza Kamata, and Issa G. Shivji, published by Mkuki na Nyota in Dar es Salaam. See https://www.mkukinanyota.com/product/development-as-rebellion-a-biography-of-julius-nyerere/.

8. https://en.wikipedia.org/wiki/Books_published_per_country_per_year.

9. The great Rabindranath Tagore, so sensitive to the human condition, especially that of women, nevertheless in his classic novel *Home and Away* puts this into the mouth of his protagonist Nikhil: "Had he been born in the wilds of Africa he would have spent a glorious time inventing argument after argument to prove that cannibalism is the best means of promoting true communion between man and man." Rabindranath Tagore, *The Home and the World*, trans. Surendranath Tagore (London: Macmillan, 1919), Chapter 10. Available at https://terebess.hu/english/tagore17b.html.

10. Edward Gibbon, *The Decline and Fall of the Roman Empire* (New York: Simon and Schuster Pocket Book, 1962, rpt 1972), 114. See also, http://louiswerner.com/new-blog/2019/11/27/why-does-philip-the-arab-remind-me-of-another-pretender-to-the-throne.

11. See, for example, Eamon Duffy, "In defence of Thomas More," https://www.the-tls.co.uk/articles/in-defence-of-thomas-more-eamon-duffy/.

12. Gabriel Garcia Marquez, *Living to Tell the Tale* (New York: Knopf, 2003).

12 LAWRENCE DURRELL AND I: THE VIEW ACROSS THE STREET

1. Lawrence Durrell, *Justine* (New York: Dutton Pocket Books, 1961). Passages quoted in this chapter are from this edition.

2. Evelyn Waugh, *A Tourist in Africa* (Boston: Little, Brown, 1960).

3. Ian S. MacNiven, *Lawrence Durrell: A Biography* (London: Faber & Faber, 1998).

4. Edward Said, *Out of Place* (New York: Knopf, 1999).

5. E. M. Forster, *A Passage to India* (New York: Harcourt, Brace and Company, 1924), 218-219.

6. M.G. Vassanji: *Uhuru Street* (Toronto: McClelland & Stewart, 1992); *The Gunny Sack* (Toronto: Doubleday Canada, 1989); *The Book of Secrets* (Toronto: McClelland & Stewart, 1994).

7. Some years ago I was hosted in Portugal by another former resident of Dar who informed me that Mr. Maundrill had come to his home one day, met his parents, and then encouraged him to apply to the London School of Economics, and even offered to pay his expenses. A life changed thereby.

13 WHOSE WAR? A BLASPHEMOUS SUGGESTION

1. The Dar es Salaam war cemeteries are discussed on the website of the Commonwealth War Graves Commission: https://www.cwgc.org.

2. *The Book of Secrets*, 1994.

3. Francis Brett Young, *Marching on Tanga* (London: W. Collins & Sons, 1917). There are several "facsimile reprint" editions available.

4. "Don Cherry sparks online backlash for comments on immigrants, Remembrance Day," The Canadian Press, November 10, 2019, https://www.cbc.ca/sports/hockey/nhl/don-cherry-sparks-online-backlash-1.5354835.

5. "The African soldiers dragged into Europe's War," BBC News, July 3, 2015, https://www.bbc.com/news/magazine-33329661.

14 A NEW DISPENSATION? AFTER GEORGE FLOYD

1. One of them, Nurjehan Aziz, now runs Mawenzi House, an offshoot of TSAR.

2. Arun Prabha Mukherjee, *Oppositional Aesthetics* (Toronto: TSAR, 1994).

3. A recent article in the *NYRB* discussed its former favourite author V. S. Naipaul's racist attitudes in some of his works. But calls of racism against this author have been around for a few decades now; they were just not heard in the mainstream, as it kept showering accolades on the author (who was undoubtedly a brilliant stylist). "How could it be," says

Howard W. French, "... that almost no mainstream [discussion] of this novel [*Bend in the River*] pointed out that saying Africans were eager to jump into ships of slave traders was objectionable and not remotely true?" Howard W. French, *NYRB* May 25, 2023, 60.

4. Among those who called out bias on the arts and academic scene were Marlene Nourbese Philip, Nigel Thomas, Alok Mukherjee, Arun Prabha Mukherjee, Himani Bannerji, and Arnold Itwaru. Of course, there were many others who protested among themselves whenever a prize was announced, for example.

5. The American philosopher Charles W. Mills, facing a similar situation, is reported to have quipped, "If you go to a meeting of the American Philosophical Association, you have to put on dark glasses, or else you'll get snow blindedness from the expanse of white faces." "Charles W. Mills, Philosopher of Race and Liberalism, Dies at 70," *The New York Times*, September 29, 2021.

6. See Ben Radley, "Who wants to hear about White Saviourism gone wrong?" *African Arguments*, March 8, 2023, https://africanarguments.org/2023/03/cobalt-red-who-wants-to-hear-about-white-saviourism-gone-wrong/.

7. See John McWhorter (newsletter), "Harvard, Herschel Walker and 'Tokenism,'" *The New York Times*, November 29, 2022, https://www.nytimes.com/2022/11/29/opinion/herschel-walker.html.

8. Ivens, Martin, "Three centuries of diversity: Paul Mendez on The Cambridge History of Black and Asian British Writing," *The Times Literary Supplement*, March 19, 2021.

9. Jay Caspian Kang, "The Myth of Asian American Identity," *The New York Times Magazine*, October 5, 2021, https://www.nytimes.com/2021/10/05/magazine/asian-american-identity.html.

10. "As Mukherjee wrote in the introduction to her 1985 short-story collection *Darkness*: 'If I may put it in its harshest terms, in Canada, I was frequently taken for a prostitute or shoplifter.'" https://www.encyclopedia.com/arts/educational-magazines/mukherjee-bharati-1940-0.

11. My work has been published in Kenya, and I have visited more than a dozen schools, given readings, and lectured at the two major universities in Nairobi. Yet I have never been invited to the annual African literary festival that takes place in Nairobi. I take it that with my brown skin I would be an embarrassment.

15 CINDERELLA ON THE OUTSIDE

1. City of Surrey (website), https://www.surrey.ca/about-surrey/diversity-inclusion, accessed August 4, 2023.
2. "Brampton" (Wikipedia entry), https://en.wikipedia.org/wiki/Brampton#Demographics, accessed August 4, 2023.
3. World Population Review, "Mississauga Population 2023," https://worldpopulationreview.com/world-cities/mississauga-population, accessed August 4, 2023.

Acknowledgements

This book has emerged, after numerous revisions, from lectures given over the years in various cities—in Canada, Kenya, South Africa, India, the US, and UK. I would like to thank my publishers, Doubleday Canada, in particular Amy Black, for allowing these thoughts and observations to finally appear in the present form. Also Kiara Kent and Ward Hawkes for their probing editorial comments, and Ward especially for his thoroughness and care during production; Melanie Little, as before, for her astute editorial eye and her helpful observations; and Carolyn Forde, my agent, for her encouragement. I would also like to thank Arun Prabha Mukherjee, Cecil Foster, David Staines, and Donna Bailey Nurse for reading the manuscript in its rough and tentative form; and Rahul Varma, Nigel Thomas, and Ali Adil Khan for readily responding to my queries; also Alok Bhalla of Delhi for enlightening discussions on Gandhi. There have been many, many others with whom I have been involved in joint projects and discussions, which have added to my understanding of the issues discussed in this volume. Finally I thank Nurjehan for listening, for her patient feedback, her research, and her advice.

M.G. VASSANJI won the Giller Prize for his novels *The Book of Secrets* and *The In-Between World of Vikram Lall*, and the Governor General's Literary Award for Non-Fiction for *A Place Within: Rediscovering India*. His novel *The Assassin's Song* was shortlisted for the Giller Prize and the Governor General's Literary Award for Fiction. His novel *Nostalgia* was a finalist in Canada Reads in 2017. His latest novel is *Everything There Is*.